For Carol Buhler
who started the
Pinckney school, i   u.

Frieda F. Rowe
11-9-71

Wonderful Old
LAWRENCE

Elfriede Fischer Rowe

The World Company
Lawrence, Kansas
1971

— FOREWORD —

These stories were written to share with others a few of my personal experiences, and to create a printed record of some facets of life in early Lawrence. The historical information has been obtained by careful research, and it is hoped it can be used as a true record. All except two of the articles have been printed in the Lawrence Journal-World.

Numerous readers have urged that the articles be preserved in a book.

The first article to appear in the Journal-World was written impulsively after reading of an event printed in the paper, which stirred up recollections of happy experiences some fifty odd years ago. Without telling anyone, I sent it to the Journal-World. The contents of the letter of acknowledgment from editor Dolph Simons meant more to me than the accompanying check.

In recounting the events and experiences, I have attempted to describe the happy and irresponsible days when about our only serious thoughts were to look forward eagerly to the next day's new adventure. Our world was peopled with friendly folks regardless of race, color or religious beliefs. We lived by the rules of our home without question and we never felt a generation gap. The idea was never planted in our minds.

Lawrence people and University people were on common ground; a wonderfully rewarding relationship.

Younger readers may see that grandparents were not always as "square" as they may have been pictured in recent years.

All of those involved in the publication of this book have a deep love for Lawrence and the University of Kansas.

There is Dolph Simons, who made this publication possible. He has continued to follow a pattern established by his father, W. C. Simons, one of the founders of the Journal-World. It is much the same pattern followed by my father, merchant and civic leader Otto A. Fischer, and grandparents Julius Fischer and F. W. Jaedicke, all of whom helped in the building of Lawrence to make it a delightful place to live and to raise and educate their families.

Then there is Theodore M. O'Leary, who in helping to edit these articles, repeated what his father, Professor R. D. O'Leary did at KU when he taught me in "Short Story" and other English courses. Museum director, Bret Waller, contributed immeasurably with his enthusiasm and helpful suggestions and encouragement. Artist Jeannot Barnes Seymour, a KU graduate, loves Lawrence and KU, and she has contributed the lively drawings which appear at the beginning of several of the chapters in this book. Her great grandfather was Isaac Newton Van Hoesen who was mayor of Lawrence in 1878. Her other great grandfather, John James Ingalls, one time U.S. Senator, gave the first commencement address at KU.

Others who either helped me remember or suggested articles, include Howard L. (Pete) Reedy and Rita Mull Reedy; Charlene Smith Fitzpatrick; Louise Broeker Young; Marcella Hetzel Arndt; Elsa Barteldes Carl; Fredo and Otto Barteldes; Julius Marks; Eva Anderson Dolbee; Maude Elliott; Pattee Sankee; and Francis Stevens.

If the reader has as much enjoyment from these stories as I have had in preparing them, then I will know my purpose has been accomplished.

This book is dedicated to my late beloved husband, Ivan Doherty Rowe.

ELFRIEDE FISCHER ROWE

The Old Fire Bell

IF YOU NEVER HEARD the fire bell when it hung in the belfry of the old Lawrence City Hall at 8th and Vermont Streets, you have missed a thrill that you could never forget.

Sixty odd years ago, fires and the spirited fire department horses excited most of the town. When a fire broke out, the bell rang out long and clear, then there would be a short pause, and then a peal for whatever ward the fire was in, then more long ringing. This would then be repeated in case you didn't get the ward number the first time. One ring was for the first ward, two for the second, and so on. No matter what you were doing, meal time or other, when that exciting, magic sound pealed forth, you dropped everything and ran to the corner to watch the horses bolt out and gallop down the street to the fire.

If the fire was in our ward, all the boys and girls in the neighborhood would run to where it was. Sometimes, when the fire was at night, a business man would be awakened by the bell and would listen for the ward number. If it wasn't in his ward, he would go back to sleep. In daytime, if it was in another ward, we would dash to the telephone and ask "Central" where it was. She always obliged by telling you.

The Lawrence Fire Department was first organized around 1875. From about 1878, firemen were housed at the same location they are now—Station No. 1, at 8th and Vermont. The old brick building had been constructed in 1869 to be used as a market. When the firemen moved in, they took the location that had been a meat market.

Early fire fighting equipment consisted of a steam boiler wagon, a reel hose wagon and a hook and ladder cart. There were two horses for the two wagons—the steam boiler and hose wagon went together. In early times when a fire started, it was at first necessary to run to the fire station and toll the fire bell. This called out the volunteer firemen and also brought either R. Delahunty or Ad Manter with their transfer wagons, who on reaching the building, unhitched their horses and hitched them to the fire carts. "Pony" Davis used his team sometimes to go get the steam engine.

There were no water mains or fire plugs to attach the hose, but the city provided large cisterns at each intersection on Massachusetts Street and one in the middle of each block from the river to 11th Street, making the one farthest south where the A&P Market now stands. Other cisterns, as ex-Fire Chief Paul Ingels recalls, were located at the Union Pacific depot; 11th and Kentucky in the center of the street; and 7th and Louisiana. These cisterns were kept full at all times and the water was hauled in tanks from the river by Milt Hays and Frank Cosley until 1880. Then the Iron Foundry pumped the water from the river as far as Sam Walker's livery stable (believed to have been on the east side of the 600 block on New Hampshire Street), where big tanks were kept full of water for the cisterns. These cisterns were kept available even after we had a "water works".

In our childhood, fire-fighting and the equipment had been improved upon somewhat. There were four beautiful, spirited horses kept at the fire station then. According to ex-Fire Chief Paul Ingels, Rock and Rowdy were on the hose wagon, and Johnnie and George on the ladder wagon. Fire Chief Reinisch drove Frank harnessed to his buggy, which was kept at his tin shop during the day. The name of each horse was above his stall. The horses were kept partly harnessed. There was what was called the "drop harness" system and when the horses were led out to the wagons, the harness would drop into place.

The fire bell and the fire department had about equal fascination. When you walked to town and reached Central Park, you stayed on the north side of the street. First you crossed the street from the park and stopped at Charlie Schultz' blacksmith shop. It was on the northeast corner of 8th and Kentucky. You lingered there to watch Mr. Schultz shoe horses. As he shod the fire department horses too, you sometimes saw Rock or Rowdy getting new shoes. They were our favorites.

After Lawrence had brick paving, in the summer, the fire horses wore rubber shoes so that the impact of shoe on pavement cushioned the horses feet and took the jar off of them. In the winter, the regular steel shoes were put on by Mr. Schultz, so the horses' feet could take hold on icy paving. Sometimes in winter, the sparks flew if they were brought up sharply or in turning a corner fast. Mr. Schultz and his father made the bodies of the hose wagons. He was also a volunteer fireman.

Next door to Mr. Schultz, was the fire station, and you were always hopeful and yet apprehensive that the spring-operated door would burst open as you were going by, and the horses bolt out. So you scampered across, not wasting any time loitering there. If in summer, the doors were open, you lingered long, looking in and hoping to be invited in to pet the horses. Quite often you were successful. I don't recall an opportunity to climb up on a wagon like youngsters in later years have enjoyed. Anyway, our main interest was in the horses. It was not until 1915 that the Fire Department became entirely motorized.

The fire chief, William Reinisch, fascinated and awed us. He was a volunteer from 1894 until 1920. He owned and operated a tin shop and would drive his galloping horse and buggy to the fire. He believed in the old German idea of discipline and you were always aware that he was running the show. When he would get up on a ladder with a hose, he would reach the top and then in a booming voice, shout: "Turn it on boys." One time when a fire seemed to be gaining headway, some spectator below offered some advice on where to direct the stream of water, and the responses from Mr. Reinisch was: "Who the hell is running this fire anyway?"

In 1929 the morning after the destruction by fire of Fraternal Aid Hall almost across the street from the fire station, Chief Reinisch was standing outdoors supervising the men who were laying the hose on the street to dry it out. A good friend, reportedly Will Johns, came along and they were both viewing the remains of the building with regret, when Johns said teasingly: "And right across the street from the fire station too."

The powerful expostulations of Reinisch could be heard for some distance.

In 1920, city officials hired Mr. Reinisch to devote his full time in the service and he served the city well until he retired in 1932, when Paul Ingels replaced him.

The fire bell didn't ring just for fires. It served many other exciting and important purposes. It was a means of communication to the Lawrence citizens. In 1903 when North Lawrence residents were threatened by the Kaw River flood, the bell rang out one midnight to summon the men in south Lawrence to come to the river front and man launches and row boats to help evacuate the people in North Lawrence who were trapped by the rising water.

One time, the fire bell was rung to call out volunteer searchers for a little five-year-old boy who had wandered too far from home. When World War I was declared, the bell tolled, and when the armistice was signed, it rang out joyously and the people of Lawrence flocked to Massachusetts Street to celebrate. The bell brought out many when the old Wind-Mill on Warren Street burned, and for the destructive fire at the old Bowersock Theatre across from the Lawrence National Bank, that had been Liberty Hall, one of Lawrence's earliest buildings.

As Lawrence spread out, a louder and more penetrating noise seemed needed, and the "Wild Cat" whistle was installed at the water works. When there was a fire, it was blown to inform the fire fighters that there was plenty of water pressure and also to arouse the town.

There were lighter moments for the firemen, too. They had their social times. About 1910, they started having New Year's dinner at the station and the wives cooked the meal. At first, they invited only a handful of "special" guests — merchants on the "street" who were special friends, and always a minister. The dinners grew in popularity until finally representatives of city offices and prominent firms were invited. There were two dinners, one at noon for the "outsiders", and one at night for the firemen and their wives.

In the days of prohibition, somehow the plum pudding always had "plum" to pour over it, and there was a little left over for "cheer" for the diners. Mrs. Reinisch always made a huge fruit cake. In later years, Wagstaff's always furnished the whipping cream and Simon Hurwitz of the Lawrence Sanitary furnished the ice cream. The turkeys were raised by Graebers and then the Jackman family.

For many years, the firemen repaired children's broken toys in their spare time at the station, to be given away at Christmas time. Then there was a Firemen's Ball, at Fraternal Aid Hall (Standard Life building now). This was for a benefit fund. A fire which gutted the hall, ended that.

No doubt, children today get as excited hearing a siren and seeing the huge trucks come racing down the street, but they would have to jump on their motor bikes or in cars to be able to follow to see where the fire was.

The old bell? It remains muted and silent up on top of the tower at the 8th and Vermont Street station.

Printed in Lawrence Journal-World—June 27, 1966.

Changes In Entertaining

DID YOU EVER STOP TO WONDER about the changes in the mode of entertaining in the last fifty or sixty years? About the only thing that hasn't changed is that you still get out your best silver, glass, china and linens for a party. But there the sameness stops. Who would have dared sixty years ago, or even twenty-five years ago, to serve sherry at a women's luncheon, or at an afternoon "tea"? In fact, who would have given a bridge-luncheon then? Most of the parties started in the afternoon and the luncheon was served at the close of the party. You can rest assured, no cigarettes were smoked then by the ladies. In fact, it took until the late twenties before women were smoking in public.

The young men who smoked cigarettes in public before World War I, were considered by many as not amounting to much, and their success in life considered questionable. Anyone under twenty-one, who wanted to try out smoking, corn silks, coffee or what-have-you, usually sneaked back of the barn or shed to do it.

Teas in those early 1900's were receptions and were in some respect quite formal. You were invited to every kind of social event by written invitation. No phones then and when the first phones did come into Lawrence homes, we had two systems; the "Home" and the "Bell". One of your friends might have a Home phone and the other a Bell, and calls were not interchangeable.

When you arrived at a party, the door was usually opened by a young daughter or a friend of the family. To be asked to do this was considered quite an honor for the door-opener. In those days, you wouldn't be caught dead not wearing a hat and kid gloves to any event, and at a reception you kept your hat on. Your wraps were left in a bedroom. Young school-girl daughters and their friends assisted in the dining room at the receptions. Chairs were arranged against the wall around the dining room and you were served sitting down.

Hot chocolate was served in winter by the girls, poured from a hand-painted chocolate pot, and a spoonful of whipped cream added; tea or coffee at the other end of the table. In summer, punch (unspiked), from a punch bowl, took the place of a hot drink. The rest of the food was brought in from the kitchen on individual plates. Colored mints were a must. The rest of the food consisted of cakes, sometimes ice cream, and sometimes home-roasted, salted peanuts. Paper napkins were unheard of. Linen napkins, sometimes edged with hand-knitted or crocheted lace, or embroidered were the only things used.

Before you left the dining room, small colored ribbon tied in a flat bow, or sometimes a fresh rose-bud, was pinned to your bosom, so the assisting hostesses could see that you had been served. The color of the ribbon matched the decorations for the party.

There usually were fresh, cut flowers throughout the rooms. Carnations, roses and sweet peas seemed the most popular, and particularly carnations. After you left the dining room, you stayed on a little longer to chat. Then, with your wraps on for departure, you tarried long enough in the hall, to take your calling card from your card-case, and drop it on a silver or china calling-card holder. This was to let your hostess know you had been there. If the reception was given in honor of someone, you left two cards; one also for the honoree. If you couldn't attend the reception, you sent your card by mail or had someone take it, to the hostess's house, being sure that it arrived on that day, and before time for the party.

If the reception was at night, the husband and wife each left their card. Card cases were not over four or five inches long and were made of mother-of-pearl, silver, or fine kid leather. They were sometimes hooked to your belt, as was your purse sometimes. You didn't always carry both to the function.

Morning coffees were unheard of. You got acquainted with your new neighbors by making a call some afternoon and leaving your card. In later years, the cards might be eliminated, but you still called in the afternoon. Years ago, one day in the week was "calling day" and we believe it was Wednesday.

Other afternoon types of parties were "cards" and "Thimbles." "Whist" was the popular card game, although "500," "Penochle" and "Euchre" were played too. On the written invitation for these events, "Whist" or "Thimbles" as was the case, was placed in the lower right-hand corner and R.S.V.P. on the opposite side. These parties were not preceded by a luncheon or dessert, as is done now, but the food was served at the close of the party.

"Thimbles" didn't mean to bring the family darning or mending, but some dainty handwork like hemstitching, embroidery, crocheting, or knitting lace (not sweaters), hemming linen napkins, and such. When you arrived for these parties, you would leave all of your wraps, including your hat and purse, in a bedroom. Purses were not needed to hold your cigarettes, lipstick or compact powder case. There was no smoking. If you needed your handkerchief, it was sometimes carried on a special little gold clip, sometimes in the shape of a hand, that was clipped to your belt, or you just tucked it in the cuff of your sleeve.

There were no lipsticks, and when they did come in, along with compacts or loose powder, it was considered most unladylike for them to be applied any place but in the bedroom. While the party was in progress, the young school-girl assistants would sneak upstairs and try on all the elaborate hats and fur wraps, with much giggling accompanying it. Sometimes an elaborate lunch would be served at the end of the party, again by the young people; or cake and ice-cream, mints and coffee. The mints would be ordered from Wiedemanns.

The Whist parties were far different from the Bridge parties of today; the game itself for one thing. All hands were held up, none exposed. Tallies were often hand-painted, or hand-made. At one party in Lawrence, "Gibson Head" drawings were on the tallies. In Whist, one hand or deal was played at a table. The game was played similar to Bridge in the playing of the hand. However, the trump was determined by the dealer dealing until she came to the last card, which was placed face up on the table before her. Whatever the suit turned up was, was the trump suit. The dealer would then place the exposed card in her hand "when it was her time to play to the first trick." Whichever pair won the most tricks, would be the winner of that round, and that pair would progress to the next table. But not until the dainty little bell at the first table would be rung to tell you it was time to move. The winners of that round would have their tallies punched with a small hand punch for just that purpose. Whoever had the most punch holes for the afternoon, would be the high. One thing sure, moving after one hand was played, circulated the guests.

Prizes would be hand-painted dishes, a bouquet of roses or carnations, a piece of cut-glass, often a picture, but never money. The men's prizes were "beautiful etchings," or cigar holders, ash trays, and such. The prizes and winners were named in the newspaper writeup. The guest lists were sometimes mentioned too. In 1908, the late Mrs. H. B. Ober had a "500" party and the first prize was a gold hatpin, and the consolation prize a "Valentine Postal." Wallace Nutting pictures were also a popular prize when he became famous.

In the early part of the century, social affairs were always in the home. For cards, the number of tables ranged all the way from nine to twelve. Then when Ecke's Hall (above Duckwalls) and Fraternal Aid Hall (Standard Life Building now), were built, and later Wiedemann's hall, the larger parties were given at those places. Twenty-five tables were not unusual. It was around 1910 when the halls were popular. The decorations were still elaborate regardless of the size of the hall.

In the beginning, help in the kitchen at home was usually the family maid, assisted by friends of the hostess and/or the family. In the early 1900's, a very beloved negro and excellent cook by the name of Lucy Brown, became the popular cateress. She was followed by Mrs. Drisdom, Mrs. Nelson, and Mrs. Walker. Lucy Brown's two favorite main dishes were veal birds and creamed chicken in cornucopias. Oysters were used often in entertaining, particularly when the men were entertained. Sometimes Lucy would bring in her daughter, Birdie, if she needed her. As she put on elaborate affairs, she was in constant demand and her time would be engaged weeks and even months ahead.

Also, about 1925, instead of the card party prizes being wrapped, they would be left unwrapped and displayed on a table, or on the grand piano, if the hostess had one. The winners could choose which gift they wanted. High for first choice and so on. A large party would have five or six prizes displayed, such as card tables, vases, and silver pieces, maybe linen luncheon sets, etc. By this time, Auction Bridge was being played. In fact, as far back as 1912, a Bridge club in Lawrence was organized, called the "Royal Auction Bridge Club."

Night entertainment with the men? There were receptions, dinners, whist parties, dancing and "Dutch Lunches." No cocktails were served before the dinners; wine sometimes with the meal. At Dutch Lunches, (suppers), beer was served. The dances started after eight o'clock. There was a popular hall in the early years, before Ecke's and Fraternal Aid Hall, called "Frazier Hall." It was in the Ludington building, 709-711 Massachusetts Street, built after Quantrill's Raid. The first floor of the three-story brick building, was usually leased for restaurants, and the second floor was occupied by, at one time, A. Faas & Company, piano manufacturers, and the H. J. Rushmer Jewelry Store.

When Mr. Malcolm Conn was owner of the Eldridge Hotel, he had the wall between the Ludington building and the Eldridge, knocked out and a doorway made, so that one could walk through from the Eldridge on the third floor. This door and opening stayed there until the hotel was remodeled in 1925. After the dances, many guests would go to Wiedemann's for oyster stew.

Seventy-five years ago, the social center for the early German settlers was at the Turner Hall, later used by the Salvation Army, at the corner of 9th and Rhode Island streets.

And how did these people get to the parties? They either walked, rode in their carriage or hired a hack (cab), horse-drawn.

Printed in Journal-World March 11, 1964

First Lawrence City Directory

ONE HUNDRED YEARS AGO, the first Lawrence directory was printed. It is dated "1860-1861" and the only copy for public reading in these parts is in the Lawrence City Library. This one has lost its first 11 pages. It is not ordinary book size, but considerably smaller and only 53 pages in thickness.

You could buy a copy for one dollar then. Not all of the residents known to have been living in Lawrence then are listed. This was the case in some of the subsequent directories in the 1860s. A man's name might not be in the alphabetical listing, but it would appear in the firm's advertisement. From page 18 on, in the 1860 edition, the left-hand pages are devoted to advertising.

There were some articles listed that are strange to the readers today. In an ad of the firm of H. S. and L. Fillmore, such items as hoop skirts, bonnets, kid gloves, and gaiters, appear. And such materials as "morene", and if you haven't your dictionary handy, "morene" is described as a coarse stout woolen, usually watered or embossed, and "merino", a soft fabric resembling cashmere. So you can take your choice of which description "morene" fits. Then there was "DeLaines", described by Mr. Webster as a light woolen dress fabric; but "Valencia", "Lyonese", and "Debage" he did not have listed in his Collegiate Dictionary. One store advertised "Yankee Notions", but we were left in the dark as to what they were, as they were not listed in the ad.

In the classified listings for 1860-'61, 19 attorneys were doing business. Lawrence has always had many attorneys. This probably can be accounted for by the fact that there were so many claims in the early years. Any transactions with the Indians, unless proper authority had been obtained from Washington, led to suits and claims and counterclaims. Squatters claims and other claims stemming from the change of Kansas from territory to a state, all added to the legal confusion of a new town.

In 1860, Lawrence also had two architectural firms; five hotels, seven dry goods stores, five civil engineers and eight brokers. Apparently the housewives didn't bake as much as one would have supposed inasmuch as you find eight bakeries listed. Only one barber was listed and he was identified as "colored".

In the 1866 directory, also priced at one dollar, there was little concern about the alphabetical order of the names, other than the first letter. One might find such order as: "Farnsworth" followed by "Frazier" and then "Fenn" and after several "FR's" and "FO's" the names "Faxon", "Farley", etc. were listed. After each person's name would be such identification as: "widow-keeps eating saloon"; "Steamboat captain-e.side Pennsylvania", "comb maker", "jailor", "ostler", "wood chopper", and many more Apparently it was thought a bachelor might be hard to locate after hours, for they did not list his residence, but where he boarded. And there were 10 boarding houses in 1866.

The residences were given numbers under 100, but many were without numbers and had such descriptions as: "Indiana, between Winthrop and Henry"; "e.side—between Pinckney and Winthrop". When the 1888 directory came out, new numbering starting in the hundreds was used.

Throughout the early years, KU students, faculty, classes and courses were given several pages in the back of each directory. The 1866 copy lists Baker University and the Deaf and Dumb Institution, with the officers. There is also a page devoted to "Baldwin City Business Guide". "Lane University—Commercial Department—Lecompton, Kansas", was given three pages.

As the years went on, the cost of directories changed; $2 and $3 in 1870's; to $6 and $8 in the early 1920's.

Printed in Lawrence Journal-World, June 20, 1961.

Home Remedies

RECOVERING FROM THE present flu bug gave us time to remember all of the home remedies used years ago, and probably now long forgotten. Just 52 years ago the worst flu epidemic in Lawrence and in the country, took the lives of scores of old and young. The only means then of combating the disease was aspirin and whiskey.

When we were young, if you were coming down with a cold, you were put to bed immediately and given a hot lemonade. This was made with the juice of a lemon, a very small amount of sugar and a tablespoon of bourbon whiskey. The glass was filled up with hot water. You had to drink it as hot as you could swallow it. Then you were buried under several layers of covers to "sweat" it out. In our house we used liquor only for medicinal purposes. Wine and beer were the pleasure drinks. Schnapps or Kümmell were taken for stomach cramps, and blackberry cordial for diarrhea.

In the winter time, we had a decanter on the sideboard filled with sticks of that clear, crystal rock candy put together with a string in the middle, and rye whiskey. A swallow of this syrupy mixture would stop coughing.

Another remedy for coughs was lemon juice and honey, or the juice of a baked onion made into a syrup. The cure we liked the best was to suck sticks of horehound candy. If you had a chest cold or sore throat, you'd get a poultice of goose grease and turpentine rubbed on your throat and chest. Then a soft white wool flannel cloth (a piece of a worn out blanket), was tied around your throat and another piece placed on your chest. Sometimes you had to take a swallow of the stuff besides. Ear ache was treated by placing a hot baked onion wrapped in a cloth over the ear and on top of that a hot water bottle.

Arnica was used by my grandmother to rub on affected parts for rheumatism.

Poison ivy was treated with wood ashes rubbed over the rash. That dried up the blisters. We had a yard man who chewed tobacco all of the time he worked. One day a wasp stung him. He dropped his tools, spit in his hand and rubbed the sting. Then he reached down and took some soft loose dirt and rubbed that on the sting. He said he never had any after effects from any insect sting.

Vitamins were unknown in those days, at least to the layman. Oranges were not continuously in the markets as now. A half dozen oranges placed with your birthday packages were a treat and not a necessary breakfast drink. In wintertime, we had to take a tablespoon of cod liver oil once a day. And what a battle that brought on.

When we were recovering from any illness, our Grandmother Fischer would make vegetable soup in a tall, black, iron kettle. She had two special enamel buckets with lids that she delivered the soup in. The grey one held about a quart and the white with blue trim, held two quarts. We got the smaller one if she had friends who were also ailing. Oatmeal cookies packed in a shoe box came along with the soup.

I recall many times in my childhood when old Dr. F. D. Morse would stop by our house and ask Mother if she could spare a bottle of wine for Mrs. So and So, who needed wine to give her an appetite and strength. He claimed rich, red, wine improved the blood. Grandfather Jaedicke believed in the old adage of "An apple a day keeps the doctor away". It seemed that every morning of the world he would drink a cup of hot water and eat a Jonathan apple. We always had three barrels of apples in the cellar — Jonathan, York Imperial and Grimes Golden. He would sit in our big kitchen at a small marble-top table at the window and peel and cut the apple in quarter sections. The marble top had come out of the Lawrence National Bank when they remodeled their counters. Then he would have breakfast in the dining room —the same breakfast year after year as long as I can remember— a soft boiled egg, eaten Continental style, home made bread and jelly, coffee with cream. He would finish off with a piece of Kuchen (coffee cake thickly covered with sugar and butter), dunked in his coffee.

Our coffee was always ground at home. The only variation from this normal diet was bacon added a few mornings in the week. My father varied this menu by finishing up with some limburger cheese that Mother kept in a covered butter dish. But the smell always came across the table when the lid was lifted.

Some of our friends had to drink calico tea and sassafras tea, but we never had it at home. A friend whose father was a doctor, recalled that her mother, over the protests of the father, insisted the children wear a small cloth bag around their necks. It was filled with evil smelling asafetida to keep them from having spasms. The bag was hidden inside their clothes, but you didn't need to see it to know they were wearing one.

Another remedy used several years ago for flu, was prescribed by a local physician, now deceased. You placed three tea bags in a cup, poured boiling water over them, let stand for one minute by the clock, poured off the water and refilled the cup with boiling water and let steep for three minutes. With this you could nibble a piece of bread that had been toasted in the oven until it was a dark brown, almost burned.

Alcohol rubs and sponging the body were the only means besides aspirin to reduce high fever.

One of the biggest changes over the years is the doctor prescribing over the phone. You always looked forward to the doctor's call. You just seemed to feel better from that visit, even before the medicine was taken. The first thing the doctor had you do, was to stick out your tongue. The idea I suppose was to decide how bad off you were by the thickness of the coat on it. Then the thermometer came next and the pulse taking.

In those early years, it was required by law that a contagious disease sign be posted near the front door. A member of the police department came to tack on the sign. The color of the card plus large black lettering, told you whether it was measles, chicken pox or whatever. As children, if we saw one of these signs posted, we would scamper across the street to avoid going close to the house. But sometimes we would be real daring and walk past, holding our breath and our noses so as not to catch the germ.

Hospitals in the early years were established in former homes. Some of the Lawrence doctors installed a hospital in their own homes. Dr. W. C. McConnell lived where the Ship Winter parking lot is, across the street from Fritz Company. He maintained his hospital in the home. Dr. G. W. Jones used the second floor of his home at 1201 Ohio. The family living quarters were on the first floor. The hospital and the family shared the same kitchen on the first floor. There was a shortage of good nurses at one time, and Dr. Jones conducted a training school for nurses, probably the first one in Kansas.

Dr. C. J. Simmons used the Jacob House home at 805 Ohio, after the House family sold it. Dr. A. J. Anderson's hospital was on the northwest outskirts of Lawrence, on Michigan street where the row of pine trees are still there. From there, his next location was at 1501 Pennsylvania, the A. H. Turney home now. Dr. John Outland, the former KU football star, was a surgeon in Kansas City and he operated in Lawrence for Dr. Anderson.

The hospital rooms were quite spare—bare wooden floors, but kept spotless. The high ceilings made the rooms seem even larger. Two biblical pictures hung on the walls of one of the rooms, one of Christ that looked across the room at you every time your eyes were open. The operating room was upstairs. How the patients were carried down those steep steps has remained a mystery. It is recalled, the day you came home from that hospital, you came by car and a chair was brought out to the car and you were carried in sitting on the chair.

Dr. H. T. Jones and Dr. E. R. Keith took most of their patients to Simmons hospital. It was the largest one. It is not recalled where Dr. H. L. Chambers took his patients.

Haskell Institute had its own hospital on the grounds. The University of Kansas first hospital, I believe, was about 1920 and it was located in the 1400 block on Tennessee on the east side. The first city hospital was in the old Judge Barker home. It was a large frame structure that stood north of the present Lawrence Memorial hospital. It was at about 100 Maine. Lawrence now enjoys a baseball diamond that took its place.

All of this was a far cry from the ultra modern hospitals and medicines of today. The use of the newer facilities, without a doubt, are reasons why some of us are still here.

Printed in Lawrence Journal-World, Dec. 13, 1968

Telephone Numbers

TELEPHONE NUMBERS seem to be getting longer and longer. Years ago, you didn't have a telephone number. When you wanted to talk to a subscriber, you told the operator you wanted to talk to Mr. So and So. She had the list of subscribers printed on a cardboard tacked on the wall near the switchboard. She would refer to that and call your party. And we didn't call her, "Operator". We called her, "Central". Reference was made to ring "Central Office" to place calls, so that probably was the origin of "Central".

Lawrence had its first phone in 1877. A member of the Ridenour-Baker wholesale grocery company brought back from the east, two telephones of the type invented the year before by Alexander Graham Bell. These phones were connected to a private telegraph line that ran between the wholesale house and a small packing house belonging to the company. Then on January 8, 1878, "the instruments were connected to a line between Chester's Drug Store and Professor Snow's laboratory" at the University of Kansas where they were used for demonstrations. E. P. Chester's drug store was located at 711 Massachusetts Street.

In 1881, the Merchants Telephone and Telegraph Company was established in an upstairs room at 733 Massachusetts Street and the Central Office was open from 6:00 a.m. to 10:30 p.m. "Conversation can be carried on at any time between those hours." There were 28 subscribers.

The earliest published telephone directory we can find was dated September 1, 1885. However, there apparently was one published before that date. The 1885 issue was 8x5 inches and hardly one-half an inch thick. It was published by the Missouri & Kansas Telephone Company in Kansas City, Missouri, and the Lawrence directory was inserted in about the middle of the book, along with Leavenworth, Atchison, and other towns. On the inside cover of the September 1, 1885 issue was printed the following: "Missouri & Kansas Telephone Co. General Telephone directory—Kansas City and Connected Lines. Destroy all Previous Issues. Call *Number* instead of name." Advertisements were printed on the narrow borders of each page. They were all of Kansas City firms with the exception of Wilder Brothers Shirt Factory. It was on a separate page on the left side of the first page of the Lawrence subscribers.

There was no classified section. The first classified directory for Lawrence was printed in 1922 and the pages were pink.

In the 1885 directory, instructions were given to subscribers: "To call—give the crank one quick turn" and "When finished, party who called for connection, hang up and give crank one quick turn, as a signal to Central Office to disconnect wires."

The phones at that time were wall phones with wooden backs. There was a black crank on the right hand side of the wooden box that held the wires. You turned the crank, with receiver on hook, to signal for the operator. Further instructions were to "Talk close to the Transmitter and in your natural voice" —"Ring off when through"—"Give operator the figures of the number you call for separately, as one-four-one-six instead of fourteen hundred and sixteen."

On a country line, (Tonganoxie was in the early directories), you didn't have to go through a central office, if the party you were calling was on your particular party line. Neighbors were all on the same party line.

You could ring your number direct. You would ring, with the receiver down, so many times, like one long ring and then a short one, or perhaps one long and two short—whatever number and type of rings the party had assigned to him. You could hear the rings whenever a call was made, but you did not answer unless it was your particular ring. If you lifted the receiver, you could hear all of the conversations going on. Sometimes so many of the receivers would be off the hook with listeners, it would be difficult for the original two parties to hear each other. This was particularly true if it were known someone was ill, or about to have a baby.

Following the wooden wall phones, came the heavy desk upright, black only, kind. Then the cradle type, but also black only and the receivers were very heavy to hold.

Very few homes had phones at first. In fact, in 1898 when F. C. Penfield, uncle of Dr. H. Penfield Jones, was manager of the Lawrence phone company, the directory had this entry: "A house telephone enables you to make engagements or put them off; to order groceries, call the doctor, turn in a fire alarm or call the police; gives you a chance to let your wife know what time you will be home to dinner. All for Ten Cents a day."

When phone numbers were put into use, they started with the digit one. As more businesses installed phones, they wanted to keep their same number for the directory. However, if a residence subscriber or business moved to another location, they didn't get to keep their old number. Some of the numbers in the 1890's that were kept for years, were: "1-Kasold's West End Grocers, (Goble's now, 547 Indiana); 48-Lawrence Journal Company; 3-Pendleton, W. H. Grocer, 86 Massachusetts; 2-State University School-Adam, S. of limits; 19-Selig, A. L. Ins. agt.—Cor. Henry and Mass.; 70-Lawrence National Bank, Corner Winthrop; 30-Merchants National Bank-Merchants Bank Bldg.; 161-3-Mitchell, A. C. Residence-821 Miss. (3 designated 3 rings-party line); 170-Reedy Bros. cider and vinegar-East Warren; 93-Barteldes, F. & Co., wholesale seeds—102 Mass.; 178-Jaedicke, F. W. Hardware Store, 724 Mass.; 236-Smithmeyer, F. H. 801 Indiana; 203-Ober Clothing, 821 Mass."

In 1918, party lines were designated by a color, black, blue, red, and white; i.e. 2180-blue. Then colors were dropped and letters were used: 1215-red changed to 1215-J. Also in 1918, "2700-Kans. Univ. Private branch exchange" was listed in the directory. Now K.U. is listed as UN 4-2700. For 50 years the University had the number 2700.

By 1905, Lawrence had two telephone companies. The Missouri and Kansas Tel. Company had moved into their new brick building at 734 Vermont Street. A new independent company owned by the Kansas City Long Distance Tel. Co., was in a new 2-story building across the street. While the two companies were in operation, many business houses had to have both systems. You could only call those subscribers on each system. At home, if you wanted to call someone on the other system, you had to go over to a neighbor who was on that other system, and use his phone to call. Both companies seemed to prosper, but World War I forced the two systems to merge. In 1917, the Missouri and Kansas Tel. company took over the Kansas City Long Distance Tel. Co. Nine years later, Southwestern Bell absorbed the Missouri and Kansas Tel. Company.

Long distance calling was not used extensively at first. To begin with, you had to go to the Central Office to place your call and then stand up to talk. Western Union telegrams were used by business and for personal use. Direct telephone lines for out of town talking, were not in existence. Phone calls had to be relayed from station to station across the country. Sometimes if there was a heavy storm at some distant point, the connections would be so poor the calls were either re-routed or the operators would take the message and relay it along the lines.

With the advent of World War II, the urgency of getting things going in a hurry, brought long distance telephone service to the front. Like many other things, priority on phone calls came into being. Sunflower Ordnance Works had priority No. 2. The Manhattan Project (H Bomb), had No. 1. This meant that all long distance calls coming into or going out of Sunflower were put through before any personal or business calls could be completed. Conference hookups came into use. Recording of conversations between army and civilians over these hookups were made. Sometimes these mechanics failed. Secretaries would be called in to take down as much as possible by shorthand in case of mechanical failures.

Before the advent of the dial system in Lawrence in 1955, the telephone operator was an unsung heroine. She was the source of all information. She would give you the time of day, or the temperature. If you heard the fire bell ringing or the Wild Cat whistle at the water works, you would pick up the receiver and ask the operator where the fire was, or why was the whistle blowing. If you tried to get a friend on the phone and the operator reported the line was busy, you asked her to call you back when they had finished.

One prominent lawyer's wife had the habit of talking at great length with her friends. One day the attorney had to go out of town right away and tried to get hold of his spouse to tell her. The line was busy, and kept on being busy. Finally, in exasperation, he told the operator to cut in on the conversation and tell his wife to hang up, he wanted to talk to her. She did, and he did.

Today, about the only contact you have with a warm, friendly operator, is when you place a person to person call with her. Perhaps the time may come when that last contact will also be mechanized. We hope not.

Printed in Lawrence Journal-World, Jan. 31, 1969

The Plymouth Congregational Church Tiffany Windows

THERE HAS BEEN MUCH TALK recently about Tiffany glass and the "Tiffany" windows in the Plymouth Congregational church. Myra Summers Keeler (Mrs. Walter J. Keeler), remembers the stories told to her many years ago about them. To begin with, these beautiful leaded, stained glass, many-colored windows were purchased and shipped from a firm in England.

When plans were made in 1868 to build the new brick Plymouth church, (which now is the center part), the Ladies Social Circle of the church wanted stained glass windows instead of clear glass. However, the members of the building committee told the ladies the church could not afford them. There was no extra money to cover such an added expenditure. The ambitious building undertaking by only 140 church members was to come to around $41,000, as it was. The organ alone was to cost $2,300.

Plans for the building of the church had started in November of 1867 when the Trustees were told to prepare a plan for a church "to cost not more than $15,000", and also to prepare a plan on how to raise the money. A building committee was elected February 17, 1868, comprised of the following: Sam Kimball; S. N. Simpson; S. O. Thacher; Wm. A. Rankin; F. A. Bailey; and John G. Haskell. Wm. A. Simpson was made collector and treasurer of the church building fund.

The Ladies Social Circle women were a strong-minded and determined group. They decided they would earn the money to pay for stained glass windows. Among the group selected on the committee to raise the money, was Mrs. Lucene Allen Barker, wife of Judge Barker, and the mother of Mrs. L. N. Lewis, Mrs. Hugh Means and Mrs. Anna Barker Spencer. Mrs. Anna Barker Spencer was the mother of Mrs. Ernest E. Bayles. Their first undertaking was to save money on Church Night suppers and other social functions held at the church. Instead of hiring help to wash the dishes, they decided to do it themselves. After a meal, wash tubs were filled and the water heated on the stoves in the church. The tan-colored, homemade lye soap wasn't too easy on their hands, but that didn't stop them. The women later said, "The windows were paid for with dish water."

Then someone thought up the idea of selling cakes and pies and hot coffee to the farmers when they came to town on Saturdays to market. Several strategic spots were picked out on Massachusetts Street where they set up business on the sidewalk. One was at the corner of the present Weaver store and the other where the Masonic Temple is located. Even though they kept the coffee hot with hot bricks, their stands had to be close to the church so they could come back and forth to replenish the coffee and food. As they couldn't carry too heavy a load at a time, they worked in relays. It took many trips.

All of this effort brought in enough money to make the down payment so the windows could be shipped. The women continued to earn the full amount of the cost of the windows until the debt was paid. Unfortunately, no one seems to know what the actual cost of the windows amounted to. Hard to believe, but true, the Ladies Circle also raised the money to purchase the pulpit furniture in 1870 which came to $172.05.

The church was completed before the windows were shipped. The open window frames were boarded up to keep out the cold and rains, and services were held every Sunday. But it got pretty cold sitting through a service, what with large cracks between the boards, and sermons in those days lasted at least an hour and a half. The late Mrs. L. N. Lewis told Mrs. Keeler how her mother and some of the other resourceful ladies in the church, decided to bring a stick of wood each Sunday to help warm things up more. They were a proud group and didn't want their friends of the other churches to know about it. So they all agreed to carry the wood under their shawls. That made them look pretty bulky, and soon it was whispered around that some of these ladies were pregnant.

It took two months for the windows to get here. Upon their arrival in New York, they were shipped overland to the Ohio river, then by boat up the Ohio, Mississippi and Missouri rivers to Westport Landing, (Kansas City). The next problem was to get them to Lawrence. This time the men came to the rescue. In order to save the expense of shipping from Kansas City to Lawrence, the men organized the borrowing of wagons and horses and drivers, to bring the windows overland. And the story goes that it was the late Sam Elliott's father who was the organizer of the undertaking.

Only one small window was broken in shipping. So much wood had been used to crate the windows for their long journey, that the women were able to sell the wood and realize enough on the sale to pay for the replacement which is American glass. That window is a small one south of the organ in the sanctuary. It shows Noah's dove carrying the olive branch, suggesting new life on the earth. No one knows what the original looked like as there is no one living who saw the broken pieces.

As Louis C. Tiffany didn't start making stained glass windows until 1878, where in America this replacement was made, remains a mystery. The other windows depict the history of God and His work. Some years ago, a Sunday school teacher from Kansas City came to Lawrence and explained to a Plymouth Sunday school class the meaning of each window. This has been recorded by Mrs. Keeler for the church.

Meanwhile, the congregation enjoyed the beautiful windows until along about 1917. Then there were some who apparently were tired of looking at them each Sunday. Some thought they didn't let in enough light into the solid walnut sanctuary with its dark red cushioned pews. Others didn't like it because they couldn't see outdoors. A movement was started to consider replacing the windows with clear glass. Word somehow reached Tiffanys.

One day a representative of that firm arrived in Lawrence to inquire about their possible sale. Reverend Noble S. Elderkin who was minister then, was at a meeting in Topeka. The Tiffany representative boarded a train for Topeka and contacted Mr. Elderkin. He told him to tell his parishioners to name their price for the windows and Tiffany would pay it. Shortly afterward, at the next church night supper and meeting, Rev. Elderkin presented the Tiffany offer. He remarked that if Tiffany wanted these windows at any price, the church had something that was priceless. The members voted to keep the windows. Mrs. Keeler is convinced that Tiffany saved the windows for Plymouth church members and friends to enjoy today.

Printed in Journal-World, Aug. 30, 1967

Street Cars

IF YOU ASK OLD-TIMERS here what they remember about Lawrence
street cars, you will get many and various answers. Some remember when they hid in Marvin Grove and waited for the motorman
to start up the winding hill from the Mississippi Street shelter.
There was a sharp turn before the climb past Bailey Hall and not
much of a chance to get a run for the top. The boys would dart
out just as the motorman would get all set for the climb, then
they would unhook the trolley. This was considered great sport
for some of the teenagers.

Some would stand on a corner and wait for the motorman
to start up after discharging a passenger, then would grab the
brass bar on the back step and swing up on the step and get a
free ride. Another prank came when a bunch of students would
be riding in the car and start rocking it into dangerous angles.
Many a boy would be riding along on his bicycle when the street
car would appear. He would wait for it to pass, then peddle
furiously and catch hold of the brass bar in back and sail along,
feet off the pedals, pulled by the "trolley".

Many remember the hot summer nights before the days of
air-conditioning. You could take the "KU Loop" ride in the open
summer cars and for 5 cents would get cooled off, for a little
while at least. If you felt real rich, you would go around twice.
There was always a breeze on the Hill and when the car left the
Robinson Gymnasium switchover and headed south, you coasted
along with what seemed like wild abandon.

Those open summer cars were completely open. You boarded
them by a long step the length of the car. The seats were wooden
benches with the backs on hinges. There was a conductor, besides
a motorman, and he would walk along this long platform-step to
collect the fares. If a storm would blow up, canvas-like curtains
were lowered to the floor and fastened. It kept out the rain, but
it would get pretty muggy inside. If you were riding a summer
car on the Indiana or New Jersey Street line, when you got to the
end of the line, the motorman would take out the brass handle
used to turn on the power, and carry it to the back end. That
would then be the front. Then he would reverse the trolley and
flip over the backs of the wooden seats and again face the front.

Others remember the rides to Woodland Park in East Lawrence. County fairs were held there, besides organization picnics
and celebrations. There were horse races and baseball games to
see, besides many buildings that housed the kind of displays
offered at county fairs. There was a dance pavilion and for 5
cents a dance, old and young got real live music.

The street car didn't come quite to the park, so visitors
walked a dusty road the rest of the way. Just west of the park

was the "Haskell Pasture" where the big-name circuses performed. After going over to the Union Pacific station to watch the circus train come in, you took the street car and went to the Haskell pasture to watch them put up the big tents. This Haskell Pasture was near where the Haskell family lived.

Many remember how accommodating the motormen were in those days. If it was raining, and he passed your house, he would let you off near your front door. Or, if you watched for him from the front porch, you'd run out in front and he would let you on. One of our neighbors living in the middle of the block on Indiana Street went regularly once a week to practice for the church choir. The motorman would stop for her in front of her house, and when she returned, she got off at her front door.

One student was courting a girl living near the end of the Massachusetts Street line. On the nights the young man was calling, he took the street car. When the motorman was on the last run, as he approached the turnaround, he would clang his bell lustily to give the young man time to say goodbye. His girl would flash the lights on the front porch and that was the signal for the motorman to wait for him. Another student was dating a girl on Mississippi Street. In the summer, they would sit on the front porch in the swing. When it was time for the last run, they would watch for the car to appear and the young man would then make a dash to catch it.

Students patronized the street cars, especially on stormy days. You could stand on the sidewalk at the Round Corner Drug Store and look south to see if the KU car was coming. You could always spot a campus car, for on the front there were two large, white, wooden letters, "KU". The Phi Gams lived on the corner of Louisiana and 8th in those days. They would come streaming out of their back door, coats flying, to catch the westbound car at Indiana. The switch was there and the motorman had to get out with his iron bar to change the switch from the Indiana Street turn. On wet, cold, snowy days, the windows would be so steamed up, you couldn't see out. But you always knew when you reached the Mississippi Street shelter — that was the first KU exodus. Sometimes you had to stand in the aisle, the car would be so crowded. Someone sitting down would hold your books for you.

If the rails were icy, sand was released through a pipe that the motorman operated with his foot. Unfortunately the sand pipe was built for straight track only. So on the curve going in back of Bailey, the sander didn't do any good. When the snow fall was heavy, plows were put on the cars and the men would work all night to clear the tracks for service the next day.

Lawrence had a street railway system as far back as 1871. At that time it was horse drawn. Later the "family horse" was replaced by a team of small mules. The rails ran the length of the business district on Massachusetts Street. (That was probably as far south as the Masonic Temple). Then it ran north across the bridge to the Kansas Pacific depot—later Union Pacific. During the early 80's, the rails were extended south on Tennessee as far as 17th Street.

In the fall of 1909, "modern" street car service was put into use for downtown Lawrence. Electric power was used. For some months, cars ran only as far as McCook Field. Then April 9, 1910, the first street car load consisting of newspaper people, officials, etc., made its first trip to the top of Mount Oread. The "loop" was completed later.

Sometimes the cars carried a motorman and a conductor. Students were given jobs at 17½ cents an hour. Some who worked the 7 to 11 shift got to study on the job. Some had summer jobs, too.

The famous, handsome, Tommy Johnson, KU football quarterback, was the motorman on the Indiana Street line. He was the idol of all teenagers. Patronage on that line was heavy when Tommy was in charge.

Apparently, all of the students didn't get along too well with some of the motormen. A report in the Journal-World in 1910 told about two prominent students hopping a street car three times and refusing to pay their fare. The motorman complained to the local police and they were put in jail for "refusing to pay their fare and being impudent in general." They were kept in jail over night and were "released the next day by giving their real names." There are other former students who remember the motorman who let them ride even if they had discovered after boarding the car, that they didn't have the fare. They would simply pay him double the next time.

In the days of "Night Shirt" parades, all street cars were put in the car barn by 8 p.m., to avoid possible mischievous pranks. The shell of the car barn, by the way, is still standing. It is occupied by McCrory-Otasco at 1818 Massachusetts Street.

There were three routes for service. The main line started from 24th and Massachusetts (about two blocks south of Breezedale) and went north on Massachusetts to 7th, then east to the Santa Fe station, south on New Jersey to 13th, and east on 13th to Haskell Avenue. It turned north on Haskell to near Woodland Park. When Woodland Park was abandoned sometime in the early 1920's, the line ran out 13th Street east to Prairie. Three cars ran on the main line.

The KU run started at 8th and Massachusetts, west to Mississippi, south on Mississippi to McCook Field. There was "open track" from McCook to the top of the Hill. A double track switch was located near old Robinson Gymnasium and the cars returned the same route until the loop was completed. Then the south bound car ran on "open track" to 17th and Louisiana, going past the James E. Dykes house to Tennessee, then north on Tennessee to 11th, east on 11th to Massachusetts, and north on Massachusetts to 8th. Two cars ran on this line. Service to KU was every 15 minutes.

The Indiana run started on 8th and Massachusetts, west to Indiana, north on Indiana to 4th. Then back the same way.

In 1916, the Kaw Valley Interurban to Kansas City came into use. A contract was signed to use their tracks across the bridge to 2nd and Locust. The original bridge that accommodated the horse-drawn street cars had been destroyed by the 1903 flood. The new street car route then went east on Locust to 8th and Locust and returned the same way. You could transfer to any of the routes on your five cent original fare.

Shelter houses were put up at McCook Field; the Massachusetts Street turnaround; and 13th and Prairie. The McCook Field shelter was the most pretentious and the largest.

The street cars were very noisy. When the car turned on Indiana, the rails shrieked shrilly. It was the same on the Mississippi Street turn. Once in a while the rails would be greased, but not often enough for the residents. One can also remember the clanging of the bell, stomped with gusto by the motorman to get the right of way. Things went along like this until 1933. Then those reading the Graduate Magazine of November, 1933, read these words: "The Kansas Electric Power Company this fall discontinued its use of street cars and replaced them with busses." End of a colorful era.

Printed in Journal-World Dec. 18, 1968

School 60 Years Ago

THE FIRST DAY OF SCHOOL 60 years ago was far different than it was in Lawrence this year. To begin with, there were no pre-school or orientation trips to the school house. The only orientation in those days was when you went to a program at your older sister's room, where she "spoke a piece" or sang a song.

Your first day arrived and you wore a white bib apron over your dark school dress. It was tied with a big bow in the back. Made of organdie, the ruffles over the shoulders were either the plain material or embroidery. Your long stockings were black and your high top black or brown shoes were button or lace. Your hair was parted in the middle and a hair ribbon was tied at the end of each tight long braid. If your hair was curly, most likely the part was on one side with a fair-sized hairbow perched on top.

You walked to school with your sister or neighbor friend and when you arrived at your destination, you waited outside for the school bell to ring. (No electric bell; it was hand-swung). Then the teacher for your room told you where to form a line and you marched in twos into the building, the youngest children going in first, and so on. You were to keep in step as you marched.

The janitor had a huge bell (at least it seemed huge), and when the children were in their rooms and it was time for classes to start, he would stand outside the school house and ring it. If he saw you coming a block away, he would wait for you to get there before he rang. You would be running breathlessly and frantically for fear he might not see you and would ring and you would be tardy; a grave catastrophe. But he never failed you.

One day when this nostalgic writer reached the corner of the West End grocery, a block from the school house, she didn't know if he had already rung his bell, and rather than be tardy, she stood hesitantly, debating whether to turn back and go home. But he beckoned vehemently for you to come on, so you ran as fast as you could and when you opened the door of your class room, he was just then ringing the bell.

After school, at Pinckney, if you had a penny or two, on the way home you would stop at the West End Drug Store when Mr. Zimmerman reigned. First you passed the Kasold grocery store, then the Bartz meat market, and then Mr. Zimmerman's wonderful drug store that had some school supplies like pencils and paper, and a marvelous assortment of candies you could buy for a penny—licorice in long hollow strands; licorice whips; horehound stick candy; candy that looked like strips of bacon and was made with cocoanut and was chewey; stick candy; dumb-bells that had a ball of hard, buttery candy on each end of a round stick of wood and covered with a light coat of chocolate; jaw breakers; and suckers on a stick that had a licorace flavor. There was no bubble gum then, but one time on the way home from school we came upon some men cutting down a slippery elm tree in front of where Lannings now live. We all stopped and peeled off the bark of some chips and chewed the pulp. It was very slippery and didn't taste too good, but it was the thing to do. We also chewed tar, used for some purpose on the streets, but it wasn't a pleasant experience.

Mr. Zimmerman was always glad to see you. Sometimes Mrs. Zimmerman with a dark, long-skirted dress, was there to help him. He would never rush you to make a decision on your purchase, but he would patiently stand by with a twinkle in his eye until you made your important selection. He seemed to have a deep affection for children. He wore gold-rimmed nose glasses and a heavy gold watch chain stretched across the front of his vest. Both he and Mrs. Zimmerman were slightly on the chubby side. When you were in about the third grade at Pinckney, sometimes an admirer of the opposite sex would buy you a five cent sack of candy from Mr. Zimmerman and wait for you to walk past him on the brick sidewalk going home, and hand it to you and then run.

When new telephone wires were put up, you would linger on your way home and pick up pieces of copper wire that fell to the ground and make spectacles with them.

It is hard to remember how the teachers at Pinckney looked, but the names of some are remembered — Nellie Morris, who taught first grade, Gertrude Sellards, (years later Mrs. Joseph R. Pearson) who taught second grade; and Mamie Dillard, loved by us all, who taught the colored children, all in one room.

There is no recollection of a general assembly at any time at school. Programs were held in each grade room. On Decoration Day, one or two Civil War veterans would visit each room and tell about the Civil War. They always wore their uniforms.

When you came home from school, you always took off your white apron and put on a dark blue checked gingham one. Then you might have to practice your piano lesson for a half hour before you could go out to play.

Printed in Journal-World Sept. 3, 1962

Watkins Bank Building

DISCUSSION ON HOW TO SAVE the Watkins National Bank building, now more commonly known as "City Hall", for the people of Lawrence, prompts one to turn back the clock half a century.

But first, let's go back to 1895 when the Lawrence Memorial Album was published by joint publishers, E. S. Tucker and George O. Foster. Two pages of pictures, both exterior and interior views of the bank, are shown and we quote some of the outstanding features: "The walls are of pressed Trenton brick trimmed with figured terra cotta and Lake Superior and Cottonwood stone. One floor of the interior is finished in richly carved quartersawed white oak. Another in the exquisitely handsome curly pine of Southwest Louisiana. The lobby floors are a marble mosaic. The wainscotting of the lobbies and stairway are of marble, eight different varieties being artistically arranged."

The publishers of the Album boasted also of six fire-proof vaults, electric call bells, handsome gas and electric light fixtures on every desk. They did not mention the brass hand rails that lead up the stairs, and the plate glass windows and the beautiful colored Tiffany type leaded glass windows in the lobbies.

When the bank first opened in 1888, it stressed the accommodation of stockmen and cattle feeders. The banking business was conducted on the first floor. The second floor was occupied by the Watkins Land Mortgage Company, one of the pioneer mortgage companies of Kansas. It had "much to do with the upbuilding of the West in furnishing to deserving farmers at reasonable rates capital with which to open up and improve new and fertile lands."

In the basement were living quarters for Will Morris, the janitor. What were in the other rooms down there are unknown, because later as a youngster we were not interested nor curious enough then to find out what they housed.

The Watkins National Bank came into focus for me when I was a student at Central School, located on the southwest corner of 9th and Kentucky streets. It now houses apartments and offices. At Central School, one of my friends was Dorothy Tucker (Mrs. Harry Stucker), whose father was "Charlie" (C. H.) Tucker, cashier of the Watkins bank. Many times after school, Dorothy and I would walk up to the bank. It was the opposite direction to home for me, but I was easily persuaded to go with her, knowing what was in store.

We would walk into the south entrance or back door of the bank. Neither the outside door nor the back door leading into the bank proper, was ever locked as long as Morris was in the building. I would stand in the back of the bank near the door while Dorothy conducted what business she had with her father.

Along the back wall, was a huge supply cabinet with shelves and cubby holes. Here all the banking stationery supplies were stored—pencils, blotters with colored pictures on them, erasers, pens, calendars, rulers, letterheads and scratch pads—a school child's paradise. When we departed, we were allowed to take one yellow pencil with Watkins National Bank printed on it, and a blotter.

These blotters were very colorful and pretty. One turned up in an attic recently and it has the picture of a young Japanese girl standing reading from a scroll in one hand and a fan in the other The caption reads "The Poem". Printed also is "Copyright 1904 by Mizru Yashioa". Below the girl's feet is printed, "J. B. Watkins, Pres.; C. A. Hill, Vice Pres.; C. H. Tucker, Cashier; W. E. Hazen, Asst. Cashier—The Watkins National Bank— Lawrence, Kansas—Capital $100,000—Surplus $20,000."

Many years later, after four years in college and one year of secretarial schooling at the Lawrence Business College, then located three floors above the Lawrence National Bank, the Watkins building again came into focus for me. This time my involvement was with the Watkins Land Mortgage Company on the second floor. In those days, it apparently was the custom to go to the father to ask permission to offer his daughter a job. Mr. Thomas ("Tommy") Green, who was in charge of the office of the Mortgage Company did just that. And so I was hired as a secretary at $90. a month. It was said at the time to be the highest secretarial pay in town. Banking hours were kept, 9 to 4 and an hour for lunch, and closed on Saturdays.

The first morning I arrived for work, I thought I had stepped into Mr. Scrooge's office. Tall desks like Bob Cratchet's were lined along the north side. A door leading off to the west disclosed a small room holding three wooden secretarial desks. Large plate glass windows covered the north side. I could choose the desk I preferred, so I chose the farthest one back. I could look out in the street from there and anyone walking along on the sidewalk that I knew, I could beckon to them to come on up and see me.

A huge vault like the one in the bank, was on the west side. On the door was a colorful scene painted in oils. One roll-top desk after the other lined the south side of the room and all unoccupied except two. Mr. Watkins had a glassed-in office at the east end. And it boasted a fire place on the north. In the winter months, if Morris knew Mr. Watkins was coming down, he would have a wood fire burning. We used to sit on the sills of the front windows and watch parades march by.

When I came to the Mortgage Company to work, there were only three others employed—Miss Anna Hutt; Mr. Green; and Mr. Stanton. I was told the Watkins Mortgage Company was winding up its business. It had been in receivership.

The Watkins Land Mortgage Company in early years, sold debenture bonds to small investors throughout this country, and to many school teachers in England. The Mortgage Company had offices in London, New York and Dallas. Their money was invested in mortgages in western Kansas, Texas, and Louisiana, and were largely farm mortgages. These debentures were issued in series secured by a certain number of mortgages and in this way it gave the investor more security. Then came the depression in the 1890's and the prices of all farm crops and property plunged down. As a result, the Mortgage Company could not meet its payments and a receiver was appointed.

Later, two committees were formed; one American and one English. Mr. T. H. Chalkley was sent over from England to represent the English investors. Mr. M. Summerfield, father of Solon Summerfield, the K. U. benefactor, was a receiver. When I came along, the liquidation was in the process of completion. Mr. Watkins was determined that the investors were to be paid back their principal, 100%, and it took many years to accomplish this.

Jabez Bunting Watkins was a small, stooped man, with piercing eyes. He came to the office only occasionally. When he died in 1921, Mrs. Watkins had the responsibility of carrying on his wishes. She was well qualified to do so as she had been his secretary before they were married, and she knew everything about the business.

Mr. Green ran the office. Quality and perfection were his criteria, not only in all work, but everything the office used in stationery and equipment were of the best. He loved young people and gaiety and colorful clothes. If you arrived at the office carrying your golf bag to take to the Country Club to play after work, he would appear at your desk around two or three and insist that you leave—that there was nothing more to do that day. He was the perfect boss.

The office was dead quiet unless you were typing—rather ghostly. Mr. Stanton worked at one of the Bob Cratchet desks, but he always appeared to be busy. The phone seldom rang and Mr. Green took all the calls. There was no phone at our end of the building. To my surprise, I found no carbon paper for office copy. There was a large press and you would put your letter typed on heavy bond paper between two sheets in a book of tissue paper sheets, use a brush to moisten the tissue and turn the wheel of the press. A copy of the letter would come off on the tissue sheet. There was a special kind of typewriter ribbon used to do this. The tissue sheets were in bound books and were stored like books.

Will Morris kept the office spotless. He was a very fine looking Negro and an immaculate dresser. When he smiled, he showed a mouthful of beautiful gold teeth extending all across the front of his mouth. We had linen towels in the wash room. Coffee breaks were unheard of then, but in the summer, when it was very hot, (no air conditioning, but ceiling fans), Morris would appear in a white waiter's jacket. He'd set up a table with a white linen tea cloth and serve us punch from a large crystal punch bowl resting on a silver tray, ladling it out with a silver ladle into glass punch cups. We would stand around the table, sipping punch and nibbling on home made cookies. Some recall that in early times, when the bank stockholders held their annual meeting in the basement of the bank, Morris would put on a turkey dinner and some of the young daughters of the officers, helped serve. When he wore the white jacket, Morris always wore a long narrow black ribbon around his neck which held his eye glasses. These were the kind that folded up and would spring open when a catch was released. They were rimless and you pinched them on the bridge of your nose to hold them on.

The long, plate glass windows were kept sparkling clean. In fact, so clean, you could scarcely tell if the windows were open or closed.

Mr. Green had one bad habit. He chewed tobacco. Usually the first thing in the morning he would come in and sit on the window ledge and visit a little. If the window was open, he might get rid of the excess tobacco juice through the open window. One such morning, after he walked out, I felt chilly and got up and closed the window. Mr. Green had an after-thought and came back in. He didn't see that the window was closed. You can guess the rest. Morris was called in haste to wash things off.

There was a back stairs on the second floor that led to the bank. Mr. Tucker would come up those stairs from the bank to talk business with Mr. Green. One day he came up and told us Jess Willard, the heavyweight champion, was in the bank. We tore down the stairs and into the bank lobby to stand beside Mr. Willard at the tellers window. The tall, powerfully built, fine looking man made the rest of us feel and look like pigmies. The most memorable thing about him was his huge hands.

And what does the building look like today? The marble stairs look a little worn down, the brass railing is not so shiny, the windows not so sparkling perhaps, but the building still has its air of elegance. And you walk out of it with the feeling, the "Old Girl" holds her age well and is probably good for many, many more years to come.

Printed in Journal-World, Dec. 26, 1969

Lawrence Bridges

THE TALK ABOUT another bridge in Lawrence brings to mind the history of the first one built over the Kaw River to connect the two sides of the city. Ice gorges and floods caused North Lawrence to be cut off from South Lawrence as the vicious elements partially destroyed the bridge.

The first attempt made to cross the Kaw River here by means other than a boat, occurred in the territorial days of Kansas. A ferry was established in the fall of 1855 by two men who had come to Lawrence as settlers. John Baldwin and C. W. Babcock started this enterprise. The ferry was quite primitive. It was a flat boat, propelled by means of a rope stretched across the river, and aided by the current. The need for a bridge became apparent as immigrants flocked into Lawrence. It was first thought that a bridge at Lawrence could not be erected on account of "yielding banks and quick sands of which the bed of the river was supposed to be formed". But a competent engineer was hired to investigate the possibilities, and in 1859, the Lawrence Bridge Company was chartered by an act of the Territorial Legislature prior to the admission of Kansas as a state,

In 1863, work on the construction of the bridge was going along fine when Quantrill and his raiders descended on Lawrence. A subcontractor and seven laborers were killed in that raid. Not only was that a catastrophe, but the stockholders of the bridge company lost their own properties and money. Finally the bridge was finished in December of 1863 and opened for travel at the beginning of 1864. That first bridge, predecessor of the present one, was described as "of the Howe Truss pattern", consisting of "five wooden spans resting on solid stone pieces, is 690 feet long and was built at the expense of $47,000". For many years this was the first and only bridge built across the Kansas River except at its mouth, and it drew an enormous amount of travel. Being a toll bridge, it was a very profitable investment.

In 1879, by a decision of the State Supreme Court, the charter of the Lawrence Bridge Company was annulled and the entire property was confiscated as property of the State. In the fall of 1872, preliminary steps were taken toward utilizing the water power. A stock company was formed early in 1873 to build a dam. While the building of the dam was in progress, a family by the name of Hutt, had arrived in Lawrence enroute from Iowa to Texas. As told by the late Edward Hutt of Lawrence, the family arrived in Lawrence on a Saturday. They always quit traveling at noon on Saturdays so that Mrs. Hutt, his mother, could get the washing done and other things ready to start out on Monday. They never traveled on Sunday. It was strictly observed as a day of rest and worship.

As the family crossed the bridge in their wagon, they saw the activity below them of the men building the dam. The father learned more men and wagons were needed. The pay was good; $1.50 a man for a 10-hour day to unload rocks, and $2.50 a day for a team and wagon to haul the rocks. The father decided to stay in Lawrence a few days longer than planned, to pick up a little money to help defray expenses for traveling. He was hired to drive his team. He took John, the oldest boy, to sit beside him. Soon the father realized he could earn $4.00 a day instead of the $2.50 by having John hold the reins on the horses while he unloaded the rocks. It became a family joke later that the young boy earned more money than the father.

With the completion of the dam, the bridge and the dam became closely tied with a series of disasters. During the month of December, 1873, an ice gorge that had formed on the river above the dam gave way and destroyed the flume on the north side, and carried with it a portion of the north end of the dam. In the spring of 1876, a heavy "freshet" took out two spans of the bridge and partially destroyed the dam. After that, things seemed to go along pretty well until the devastating flood of 1903. That time, the north span of the bridge was washed out and the Bowersock Mill was swept from its foundation and destroyed. For several days before this happened, crowds of people watched the river rising to a final 28 feet. No one was allowed to cross the bridge at the south end except to go across to help those on the other side. North Lawrence residents were evacuating their homes and crossing to the south side. It was finally realized the Bowersock Mill was going to be taken by the raging waters. It, too, was evacuated. An estimation of how soon it would go was made. They finally had it figured down to hours. As the word spread over town, hundreds of men, women and children congregated to watch its demise. Around noon a shout arose from the crowd as the mill cracked, moved and broke up. The crowd was showered with flour. The entire north span of the bridge went out that evening when it was struck by a house, and the crash was heard all over the city. The loss of the mill was estimated at $100,000.

The U. S. Army Engineers came from Leavenworth to help, and a pontoon bridge was considered. But after looking over the situation, it was judged impractical. Instead a ferry was operated just west of the Santa Fe depot. And this continued for about 24 days before the bridge was again in use.

There was another flood threat to bridge and dam in 1904 and again in 1908. Then in 1910, an ice gorge threatened the bridge, but it survived without damage. In the Journal-World of 1913, it was stated the old bridge was rapidly approaching an unsafe condition. A new bridge was to be built of reinforced concrete. January, 1917, the $225,000 present structure, built by

Douglas County citizens, was dedicated and opened. Then, in July of 1951, flood damaged the approach to the Kaw River bridge on the north side, but it was repaired soon after. Today, Lawrence has the Turnpike bridge as another means of crossing the river, should an emergency arise.

Lawrence Journal-World — April 11, 1968

Lawrence Bands

"To the citizens of Lawrence; Buch's Military Band wishes to state that on account of the electric light plant being out of order, that the band will have to discontinue the band concerts for an indefinite length of time, until the lights are in the park."

This article appeared in the Gazette on June 10, 1903, and had reference to the disastrous flood of that month and year. Buch's Military Band, and those before it, gave many residents a delightful evening's entertainment every summer for those who were "compelled to stay at home during the summer months". The first concert of each summer started in South Park on a Friday evening, usually around the first of June, and the concerts were alternated between South Park and Central Park.

Homeowners living near the parks always had friends sitting on their porches, steps, and porch railings, to listen to the concerts. On particularly hot nights, the women would fan themselves with fans made of cardboard with a wooden handle, advertising some merchant's wares, or those made of basket weave straw. Sometimes the hostess would serve lemonade to her guests. Many horsedrawn carriages would park along the curbing near the band, and listen to the concert.

Men, women and children strolled around the bandstand, disregarding the attacks of mosquitoes, chiggers, and June bugs with their clutching claws. You could always count on three popular pieces to be played at every concert — "Listen to the Mocking Bird"; "The Whistler and His Dog"; and John Phillip Sousa's "Stars and Stripes Forever".

* * * * *

Lawrence almost always had a band; the first one was formed in August of 1854. There were such names as Alford; F. Savage; N. Hazen; A. H. Hazen; James Sawyer; Joseph Savage; O. Wilmarth; and Harlow. When these men met in Boston to start on their journey to Kansas, they had their musical instruments with them. At the station, John Greenleaf Whittier had distributed large cards on which were printed the verse of his poem, "The Kansas Emigrants", written especially for the occasion. Someone in the group discovered that the meter of the poem corresponded

to the tune of "Auld Lang Syne", and the men immediately began
to play—

> "We cross the prairies as of old
> "The Pilgrims crossed the sea,
> "To make the West as they the East
> "The homestead of the free."

After arriving in Lawrence, these men became the nucleus
of the first musical organization in Kansas. They played national
airs, hymns and Sunday School songs. The first festive celebration
in Lawrence was July 4, 1855, and the band played in a grove
about a mile northwest of town. By the spring of 1856, the
pioneer band was well organized and some of the names that
were added to the list were, Samuel Kimball and Fred Kimball.
Gen. James Lane had the band play frequently to provide martial
music to stimulate enlistment in the volunteer militia for the protection of the town. They also played at funerals.

The band grew in numbers and prospered until 1863. In
March of that year, the Kansas Conference of the Methodist
Church was held in Lawrence. In honor of the event, the Methodist Sunday School arranged for a concert in which the band
took a prominent part. A movement then was started to secure
new instruments for the band. Gov. Charles Robinson headed a
subscription list to raise the necessary funds. A new set of silver
instruments was the result. After diligent practice, the bandsmen
assembled the evening of August 20, 1863, and gave a concert
from a platform that had been erected near the bridge, (where the
Shunganunga boulder now stands). The next day Lawrence was
destroyed by Quantrill.

"For more than a year the survivors had but little time or
heart for music, but at the time of the Price raid in October, 1864,
they went to the front as a militia band and served on the border
for two weeks", one account said.

June, 1867, the band assisted in the exercises of the first
commencement at Kansas University. On September 15, 1879,
the remaining members of the band assembled for the last time.
It was the 25th anniversary of the arrival at Lawrence of that
New England party which left Boston in 1854 singing Whittier's,
"Kansas Emigrants", and they had been called together to furnish
music for the old settler's meeting at Bismarck Grove. Some of
the members came back to Lawrence just to play that day. The
last survivor of the band was Forrest Savage.

Soon after, John H. Bell came to Lawrence in 1884, and he
organized Bell's Military Band. Mr. Bell had a music store in the
700 block on Massachusetts street. He played the trumpet, an
instrument which up to that time was rare in a band. His horn
was of French make and gave out a beautiful tone. Mr. Bell was
the father of Bonnie Bell Houston and Walter Bell. He wrote
many marches for his band, some of which were arranged for

the piano and were published. The titles of some of these are: "Intrepid Leader"; "Chicago Land Festival"; "Old Knickerbocher Jr."; and "Euphonia" which featured the tuba. They were all peppy marches. One called "Old Napper's Hick Nut Dance", was inspired by the music that was played on a banjo by an old Lawrence Negro who used to drive down the street in his wagon singing and playing his banjo. They called him "Old Napper". The Bell band eventually disbanded, due probably to the stress of business interests.

Buch's Military Band followed. Mr. John Buch taught wagon-making at Haskell Institute. He organized a brass band in 1878 with 10 friends, all Germans, who were among the early settlers. These 10 men played together until 1884. The original ones were Buch; Schneider; two Lesch brothers, two Griggs; Yeager; Biebush; Rhinehammer; and Bell. The band consisted of two drums and eight brass instruments.

By 1900, the band had grown to 28 and the members were: Leader, solo clarinet — John Buch; piccolos — Ed James, Paul Dinsmoor; clarinets — Roy Cooper, Walt Brannin, Ben Keiser, G. Leis, Al Bromelsick; cornets — Gerhert Planz, Will Dick, J. R. Topping, Will Harris, Ed Leis, Ben McFarlane, Ed Riling; altos—Harry Lander, Dick Booth, Frank Iliff, Clarence Hanscom; tenors — J. F. Davis, C. Stow, R. E. Everett; baritone — Hugo Ketels; basses — A. Planz, R. Swartz; drums — Fred Easter, O. E. Bryan, Fred Soxman.

Buch's band and the Haskell band played at the Santa Fe station, June 29, 1900, when Gov. Theodore Roosevelt of New York, vice-presidential candidate, had a 10-minute train stop here.

John Buch also had a very popular orchestra. His three sons played in it with him. John Jr. played the violin and also made violins; Louis played the violin; and Bert played the cello. Walter Bell also played in this orchestra. Every summer Bert and Walter Bell played in an orchestra at Elitch's Garden in Denver. Once Bert was an accompanist for Ignace Paderewski, famous pianist. Paderewski reportedly told him he was one of the finest accompanists he had ever had.

Walter Bell played string bass. He could arrange most any music. Walt and Bert practiced every morning in Denver with the orchestra to get ready for the concert. A young teenager used to hang around and listen to them. One day a lady called Bert and told him her son was the boy who was there every day, and she asked Bert to give him music lessons. The boy was at a difficult age and this was the only thing he seemed to be interested in. Bert taught him the violin and viola. The boy's name was Paul Whiteman.

Walter Bell left Lawrence and played in Kansas City at the Shubert Theatre and then on to San Francisco to play in the San Francisco Symphony Orchestra. Paul Whiteman formed his orchestra and when he was in San Francisco he contacted Walter Bell and persuaded him to join him and arrange all of his music for him. They toured the United States and Europe, and his orchestra played in Lawrence.

After Buch's Band broke up, there were the Haskell band, the Kansas University band and the Lawrence High School band to take its place.

Published in Journal-World May 5, 1965

Old Homes in Lawrence

LAWRENCE HAS AN AMAZING NUMBER of older homes that are still standing, occupied and in good condition.

The first house in Lawrence was built in 1854. It was a log cabin about 18 by 24 feet and erected by Clark Stearns a pro-slavery man from Missouri. The act of organizing the territories of Kansas and Nebraska passed Congress, May 30, 1854, and within a few days after that, Stearns arrived upon the ground and erected his cabin as a squatter's claim, for a farm. The New England advance pioneers found him there with his family and after they erected their tents, August 5, 1854. When they proposed to organize a town company, Stearns was an obstruction to be got rid of, and they bought him out for $500. There is a cement marker at 616 Massachusetts Street, just south of Underwoods, in front of a used car lot, and bordering the sidewalk, which reads: "Site of the first house in Lawrence, 60 feet east."

In June of the same year, Achilles B. Wade built a cabin and settled on it as a squatters claim. He later accepted $100 for his claim, and left. Wade's cabin was east of the present Water Works, on Indiana Street.

After Stearns left Lawrence, Caleb S. Pratt bought a stock of goods to put in the Stearns cabin, but before this was accomplished Paul R. Brooks and his cousin, D. H. Brooks, purchased the goods from Pratt and moved them into the building. Thus, the first cabin became the first store building in the city.

Lawrence was a city of tents at first. One type of building peculiar to Lawrence was called a "hay tent" or "A" house. These tents or "A" houses were built by setting up two rows of poles, then bringing the poles together at the top and thatching the sides with prairie hay or cotton cloth. The tents or houses were all roof and gable. The windows and doors were at the ends.

The reason they were called "A" houses was due to their shape. The opening was like the printed letter "A," and the "hay tent" name must have been derived from hay being used on the sides. These tents were long and high. Two hay tents were put up almost immediately on arrival of the emigrants — one for a boarding house, and the other for the Church or meeting house. The boarding house was run by two women who served some 150 people at $2.50 a week. Two rough boards were laid across some logs for a table and in the beginning the boarders sat on wash tubs, kegs and blocks. Both of these hay tents were also used for general shelter and sleeping quarters until the newcomers could erect something for themselves.

There were few log cabins built at first. Log cabins had never been introduced into New England so the New Englanders did not know too much about how to build them. Those that were erected were made of oak, hickory or walnut.

Sod houses too didn't come until later, although sod was sometimes used for walls for the hay tents and houses, but not for an entire structure. The houses made of other woods came after saw mills were erected. In the spring of 1858, steamboats on the Kaw brought eastern lumber and pine. In the meantime, limestone rock was used, and for mortar, limestone was burned to produced lime.

The New Englanders had little knowledge of stone, so they turned to brick. The first kiln of brick was burned in the spring of '56. The old brick plant was at the foot of Mississippi Street, if it were cut through. The pond later became Green's Lake and now belongs to the Veterans of Foreign Wars. The brick that was made here was of mud and hay and was a soft brick. The vitrified brick came later. Some of the houses I am going to speak of later are made of this soft brick.

It is surprising that these early houses were so well made and some too, quite large. But many of the early New Englanders were well equipped, both education-wise and moneywise. They came from families in the East who had means. Later, as some of the citizens would become more prosperous, particularly in the early 1870's, the man of the family wanted to give his family the best, and he would build a larger and more pretentious house. When they moved into the larger houses, they needed more furniture and much of this extra furniture was purchased at auctions that were held in Lawrence, for a while, almost regularly.

Many of the early settlers made a great deal of their furniture. They used the predominant wood, which was walnut. Lawrence had a saw mill and later a planing mill.

After the strife was over and Kansas became a state, many men left Lawrence with their families because they had accomplished the purpose of their coming. Others left because of dissatisfaction, and some because of illness or homesickness. They did not want to be burdened with household effects, or they needed money to go back, so auctions were a common and popular event in Lawrence. The men particularly attended these auctions, both as a social event and to pick up furniture to supplement what they had.

In examining the life of the women during those times, one thing stands out in reading the various diaries and articles, and that is their cheerfulness and enthusiasm. They would write letters home telling of the beauty of the prairies, the wild flowers and birds, the deer, and believe it or not, the climate. They suffered the shortage of such things as milk, butter, and eggs, to name only a few. They accepted these hardships of housekeeping without the conveniences they were used to, with a cheerful and quite often amusing comment, rather than a lament. Many substitutes were used in their cooking, where only the prairies would produce the ingredients. Some of these no doubt were used by the women living on farm claims, rather than in towns, but I have a few recipes that could have been used by them all:

Corncob Sirup — (Red ones preferred). Boil for 2 hours; strain and add 2 pounds brown sugar. Boil until thick.

Sheep Sorrel Pie — (Lemons were scarce so in a lemon pie recipe they substituted shredded pink-flowered sheep sorrel.)

Acorn Bread.

Wild Grape Dumplings.

Clover Blossom vinegar.

Cockelbur Cough Sirup.

Pea Hull Soup.

And this recipe was given for Roast Goose in 1870: "On the day before Christmas, kill a fat goose and dress it. Wash it well in a dishpan of hot soapy water. Rinse in a milk pail of cold water. Dry it thoroly and hang it up in the woodshed over night. Next morning early, mash a kettle of potatoes with cream and butter and a cup of chopped onion and lots of salt and pepper. Stuff the potatoes into the goose and sew it shut. Rub the skin over with salt and pepper and sage and put it in a not too hot oven. (No thermostats in those days.) Dip the grease up every hour or so and save for cold-on-the-lungs and shoes."

Cook books in those days weren't sticking their necks out by giving specific instructions. "Grease saved for shoes" — grease applied on the soles and sides of shoes, made them waterproof. But can you imagine how those shoes would smell in a hot, damp room?

Even back in those early days, the women worried about their weight! This was found in an old cookbook: "How to Grow Thin." "Drink as little as you can get along with comfortably, no hot drinks, no soup, no beer and only milk enough to color the lukewarm tea or coffee you drink. Eat chiefly stale bread, lean meat with such vegetables as peas, beans, lettuce in moderation. Avoid watery vegetables such as cabbage, potatoes, turnips, etc. No pastry whatever. Limit yourself to 7 hours of sleep out of the 24, and take plenty of exercise in the open air."

Here are a few beauty hints in those early cookbooks:

Face Powder

"Take 1/4 pound of wheat starch pounded fine. Sift it thru a fine sieve or a piece of lace. Add to it 8 drops of oil of rose; oil of lemon 30 drops; oil of bergamot 15 drops. Rub together thoroughly." (Bergamot is a pear-shaped orange whose rind yields an essential oil used in perfumery.)

To Remove Wrinkles

"Melt together one ounce white wax, 2 ounces strained honey and 2 ounces of the juice of lily bulbs. The foregoing melted and stirred together will remove wrinkles."

For recreation in those real early days, there was hiking, horseback riding and in the winter, skating. There were many ravines in Lawrence then, and they would be full of water. In the winter, skating was excellent and the best places were lighted with flares for skating at night. The river too, was used for big skating events. Coasting and sleighing came with the snow.

Then there was Liberty Hall, a building that was erected at the corner where the present Jayhawker Theatre building now stands. The entire second floor was one large room which was the scene of many gatherings. The room was open every afternoon and used like our community building. The churches alternated having meetings there — graduation exercises were held there, lectures, home talent and imported plays, all were held in this hall.

There are conflicting dates of when some of the old residences around Lawrence were built; however, the ones I have chosen were built from 1854 and in the 1860's. One thing that is amazing was that the houses are scattered all over the town; east, west and south of the Hill. Not like today, where several dozen houses are built at one location as a new development opens up. However, I am convinced that a great many of the very earliest houses were erected in east Lawrence, east of Massachusetts Street.

All of the houses I am writing of are on the original townsite. If you would examine the abstracts of these homes, you would find the first entry with the name of Robert Robertaille, who was a Wyandotte Indian Chief, and who represented his tribe in these transactions. It was Wyandotte land on which the emigrants settled.

The old Babcock barn at 2239 West Drive was converted into a duplex by George K. Melvin. Mr. Melvin's grandparents were early settlers. Next door north on the Melvin property is a small house built and used by the Babcocks for the servants. The Melvins use it for storage only.

At 623 Indiana, Adam Oliver brought his family from England in 1858 and to Lawrence in 1862. After Quantrill's Raid, the family went to Canada for a short time, but soon returned to Lawrence and Oliver built the house at 802 Tennessee. Many people in Lawrence think the 802 Tennessee residence was the first house of the Olivers, but the records show otherwise.

Also in the 800 block on Tennessee is 827 recently owned Mr. and Mrs. Ralph Tait. This house was built on the edge of a ravine which was later filled, leaving the first floor below the ground level. The Robert H. Miller house — 1111 East 19th

Street, was built in 1858. It was a farm home then, and remained in the Miller family until the death of a son, Vanroy, in 1952. There are many interesting stories in connection with this house and Quantrill's Raid. Leo Eller is the present owner.

The house at 743 Indiana Street was built by Hiram Towne, a well-known contractor. He built North College, which is still a memory for some of us, but only a picture to many. This house at 743 Indiana was rented by Towne to a widow Mrs. Emily Hoyt, but he reserved a room for himself.

The day of Quantrill's raid, Mrs. Hoyt's teenage son hid in the corn field in back of the house. The original house did not have the south extension on the porch, nor the bay window. The first fence around the property was wooden picket. All three lots were in the original deed. Incidentally, the taxes shown on the abstract, for the last half of 1878, were $3.85 for each lot and the lot with the house, $38.50. It is interesting to note, the taxes for this year (1960) for the same property and the same house amount to over $500, compared with $92.40 for the full year of 1878; an increase of about 550%!

The present iron fence and bay window, and the extension of the south porch, were added by F. W. Jaedicke, then gunsmith and hardware merchant, when he purchased the home in 1879. Jaedicke came to Lawrence the year after Quantrill's Raid. Since 1879, the house has remained in the Jaedicke family, being presently owned by a daughter, Mrs. Otto A. Fischer.

The house at 1008 Ohio was built by George W. Bell. It is across the street from Corbin Hall, on Ohio. The 718 Locust resident in North Lawrence was built in 1869 by A. J. Dicker and has been in the Dicker family since. Dicker came to Lawrence in 1868 and built his grocery and meat store in North Lawrence and a year later built his home east of the store in the following block. The home is now owned and occupied by Donald Dicker.

Other homes include: 1105 Rhode Island — The home of Mrs. A. B. Mitchell. It was built in 1855. 1106 Rhode Island — This house is occupied by Tom Delahunty and his sister. It was built about 1870 by Tom's father, R. Delahunty. He was in the transfer business when he came to Lawrence in 1867 and Delahunty helped haul engineering equipment for Gen. Fraser to survey the site for Fraser Hall. 702 Rhode Island — Built by Julius Fischer in 1869. He was the father of the late Otto A. Fischer, shoe merchant. Julius Fischer was one of the original 16 Germans who were sent out in 1857 from Chicago, by a German Association formed there to found the town of Eudora. The house is now owned by Wm. L. Holliday.

304 Indiana — I don't know who built this house, but it was always referred to by the old timers as the Kahoe home. This location was possibly the site of the home of Achilles B. Wade. 309 Indiana — across the street from the Kahoe house and possibly

the home of Wm. H. R. Lykins, one of the first emigrants. 323 Illinois — Built about 1870. Family by the name of Van Hoesen lived there. It is now occupied by Mrs. Katheryn Wilson Stevens who represents the 3rd generation of the Eli Wilson family to live in it.

Printed in Journal-World December 8, 1960

Our First Overland Trip To Colorado

WHAT? DRIVE TO COLORADO and back over the weekend? It used to take us that long just to get to Denver or Colorado Springs. If you reached there in three days, you were considered a good driver—and lucky with dry weather, dry roads and no tire troubles. And every year it was a new adventure to drive it.

Our first car and our first trip overland to Colorado came all in the same year. The black Chevrolet, four-door touring car, was purchased over fifty years ago from W. O. Hamilton, who had been former coach and athletic director of K. U. It was the show car at the Automobile Show in Kansas City and it was the model called the "Baby Grand". Fritz Meyn, one of K. U.'s star football players, worked for Mr. Hamilton and he taught us to drive it. The day the car was delivered, we drove the nine miles to Eudora and back. We would stop now and then and practice shifting gears and backing. When we got back to Lawrence, we dropped Fritz off at the garage and were on our own to get home. Our knees shook all the way, but we made it. That night after supper, we took the folks for a drive out in the country. (23rd Street).

There was a rule in our house that you didn't buy anything unless you had the money to pay cash for it. And that was the way the car was purchased.

Our car was different from any other one in Lawrence. It was truly the forerunner of the closed sedan that came out a year or two later. It had two demountable tops. In summer, you had the canvas top that you could put up or down, with side curtains to be snapped on when a rain storm came up. Other car owners used the side curtains in winter to keep out the cold. But for winter, we had a hard top that was put on in place of the canvas one. It had glass windows all around. It was quite something to sit comfortably on the black leather cushions and let the weather be what it may. Whichever top was not in use, was stored at the Chevrolet garage. As this glassed-in top was an innovation, Father was up for much ribbing from some of his friends, who called the car his "hearse".

Tools for the car were kept under the front seat—the spare tire was attached on the outside in the back—no trunk for luggage. Luggage space was provided by collapsible racks fastened on the running boards. No windshield wipers. The windshield was split in the middle so that you could open each part out, and get more breeze that way. In summer, you fought June bugs at night and grasshoppers in the day. There were no heaters. In winter, when we would drive to some friends in the country, or were going to Kansas City, we heated a rectangular piece of soapstone that belonged to our fireless cooker, wrapped many layers of newspapers around it and then placed it on the floor inside an automobile robe. We only had two of these, so Mother would heat two irons and wrap them the same way. Sometimes they got a little too hot, and you would smell the scorched paper and also the robe, and you worried that you might find a hole in the robe when you got to your destination.

The cruising speed overland was around twenty to twenty-five miles an hour. If you went thirty, you were really "flying". Town speed was ten to fifteen miles per hour.

When we took our first overland trip to Colorado that summer, we had been practicing overland driving by making frequent Sunday excursions to Kansas City. That took almost three hours driving each way.

We decided to take the Golden Belt route to Denver. There were other routes—the Santa Fe Trail; Rock Island Highway; Union Pacific Highway; and the Lincoln Highway. There were no road maps in those days, at least not in Lawrence. We were equipped with a Blue Book—official name: "The Automobile Official Blue Book". It was the motorist's "Bible". It was about the size of a desk dictionary and almost as thick. It was bound in leather and sold for $2.50 a volume. A friend loaned us his. There were four volumes published. We used Volume 4 — The Middle West. The entire trip to Denver was spelled out by mileage. For instance, you started "O.O", Lawrence, left-hand road immediately after crossing bridge; straight ahead passing depot on right, and so on. As you drove along, landmarks would be pointed out, such as "windmill on left, red barn, jog right, cross bridge", etc.

There were few road markers in those days, no highway signs—The Sunflower Trail, running north and south boasted, "marked with an 18-inch yellow band painted around the telephone poles".

You would drive for miles on the hot, dusty, dirt roads, and the only guide was the person holding the Blue Book on his lap and reading out loud from it. If you came to a crossroads on the prairies, your Blue Book might say, "4-corners; turn right. Go straight ahead, avoiding all cross-roads, passing depot (on right—32.7) to center of town", you were approaching.

Gasoline filling stations were unheard of. You picked out the best looking or sometimes the only garage in the town and they filled the car from five-gallon cans. All roads took you through the main street of every town. Whenever you stopped, someone of the party would walk around the car and check the tires for nails. Roads ahead and weather conditions were always discussed, and how far to the next good-size town that had a good hotel to stay over night.

That early morning in July, on our first trip, the skies looked cloudy. When we got to Manhattan, we left the main Golden Belt route to go to Clayton, Kansas, due to wheat harvesting at a ranch. The Blue Book cautioned: "This is an optional route to the Golden Belt, but is not recommended". No wiser words of caution were ever written. Ten miles out of Manhattan, a heavy rain and thunder storm blew up. We had to keep going as there was no place to stop and the road was getting slicker and the ruts deeper. We managed to slide into Riley, Kansas without chains—total population probably around 300. We were greeted by other tourists who had made it in ahead of us. The main street of Riley looked like Matt Dillon's main street of Dodge City in Gunsmoke, with not as long a main street. All structures were wooden, and a wooden roof covered the walk. The "hotel" was in the center of the block. That night, cars fared better than their drivers. They were stored in the only modern building in the town—a large garage with a cement floor.

Our room held an iron bed, the usual wash bowl, pitcher, and jar, and a towel apiece. There were no keys for the doors and the proprietor was astounded and insulted to think he was asked for one. We braced our door with a chair against the knob. Young as we were, it was pretty hard to go to sleep that night— you seemed to feel things crawling on you.

We had supper that first night at the hotel as it was the only place in town to eat. After seating ourselves, we were facing the wide open doorway where the guests entered. We were startled to see the local patrons walk up to a stand with a wash bowl on it, pour water in the bowl from a large pitcher, and proceed to wash hands and face, use a community towel, comb their hair with a community comb hanging from a chain fastened to a post that supported the roof and from which hung a small mirror, and then sit down to be served. This ritual took place before every meal.

As the rain continued the rest of that first day, by evening it was an accepted fact, if the weather did clear in the night, we still would not be able to leave Riley, even with chains until, sometime late the next day. But it rained all that night too, and no car, truck, or wagon came into the town from any direction.

We were unhappy, reluctant guests for two nights, and by noon the third day, all the travelers were desperate. We were restless and bored—no radios, no papers, no magazines. We were completely isolated. To our knowledge, no one had come into the town from any direction. We spent the daytime walking over to the garage and eyeing with envy the clean surroundings for our cars, and threatening to sleep in them if we didn't get out of town soon. Then we would stand around the corner where all traffic had to pass, hoping to see someone drive into town so we could ask about the roads. Finally, around ten o'clock the third day, a truck plowed into town and the driver told us he thought we might make it if our chains would hold us in the deep ruts, and if we didn't have to pass anyone coming towards us. We started out in a sort of parade—there were three cars going west, and fortunately we were not the lead car. However, a few miles out the roads improved.

Two days later found us in Colby, Kansas and we were introduced to the rope fire escape. The stone hotel where we stayed, was built like a fortress. Our rooms were on the second floor. We asked about the huge, thick rope that was fastened to a large iron ring driven in the wall by the window. We were told that was our fire escape and in case of fire, to throw the rope out the window and slide down the rope. Fortunately, no fire broke out.

Our Blue Book for the Colby to Denver route, via Limon, Colorado, told us: "Leaving Colby we proceed westward, following the line of the railroad through a country that has for a great many years been devoted largely to the raising of cattle. It is necessary to stop the machine a number of times in order to open fences which are kept closed on account of the grazing cattle. Prairie dog towns are a common sight along the way, a small specie of owl living in the same holes with the prairie dogs." And out of Stratton, Colorado, "Wire gate straight ahead"— "4-corners—road ahead grass grown".

Our meals enroute were picnic style at noon, and a good hot dinner at night. The meals at night were usually excellent and home cooked tasting. At noons we would either stop at a grocery store if the local cafe didn't look too inviting, or clean, and buy crackers, bread, cheese or sausage, fruit, and make sandwiches and eat in the town park or under a shady tree in the country. The farther west you went, the trees became more scarce and so a park in town was chosen. It was cooler and water was available. Farther west on the prairies, after an upset stomach, we learned to ask if their water was alkali. If so, we would squeeze lemon juice in the glass of water, if we just had to have a drink at that town. We often stopped at school houses for our picnic lunch and to use their facilities for comfort, if the towns were too far away. Most of the towns then were about fifteen miles apart, and we would watch for the water towers—sometimes we could see them for ten or fifteen miles.

Many a storm cloud was watched anxiously as we rode along those hot, sandy prairie roads, particularly in eastern Colorado. One afternoon, the black, swirling, churning clouds caused us to get out and snap on the side curtains and then it looked so bad, we decided to sit in a ditch and wait for the worst. The storm veered north and all we got was hail, wind and some rain. With the side curtains on, it would get pretty steamy and hot inside.

It was no uncommon sight to see jack rabbits and coyotes all through western Kansas and eastern Colorado. Grasshoppers were plentiful and big. In some sections, the roads were literally covered with them. Winding, wooded roads through Kansas, seeing all sorts of wild birds, sometimes snakes, many wild flowers, gave each traveler a lesson in natural history. When the prairies were in bloom, the memory of the coloring still stays with us. Windmills were plentiful. There were few fences in eastern Colorado. Many black-eyed Susans took away the bleakness of the prairies with their bright yellow blossoms. You met few travelers. If someone did pass you along the route, you most likely would meet them again in the next town at the drug store getting a soda.

After we had driven across the state about 400 miles, we began to notice the car didn't pick up very well. It seemed to lose power, and it didn't take the hills as fast. We stopped at the next town to have the car checked, only to be told the car was all right, but that we were climbing to higher altitude.

We never drove after dark unless we had read our Blue Book wrong. Lights on the cars were not very bright, the roads were not marked and you couldn't see to read your directions. If you were unlucky enough to have to drive after dark, your only guide to a town was to watch for the glow against the dark sky.

After two glorious weeks in the mountains, we had hopes of an uneventful trip home. Not so. We left Denver around noon. About ten miles east of the city, we came upon the aftermath of a cloudburst and flash flood. A flash flood lake confronted us. The Union Pacific railroad tracks bordered the highway—they were built up high above the road. We were told the only way to get past the lake of water was to climb up that incline and drive down the track—and we did just that. The men helped each other lift each car over one rail—the women drove, and we straddled it and bumped over each tie to dry land. Not only that, but the cars had to be braced going up and coming down the incline. From then on, it was clear "sailing" home.

Despite the many unpredictable crises and delays, we were ready to start out the next summer for another adventure.

Lawrence Journal-World — August 22, 1966

Spring-Gardens

ANNUALLY, WITH APRIL AND MAY showers, temperatures on the rise, trees leafing out and fruit trees blooming, our thoughts turn to gardening and other activities associated with spring.

Back in the old days nearly everybody had a garden — both vegetable and flower. Flower planning and planting was the responsibility of the women in the family, and the vegetables were left to the men. The vegetable garden covered a small plot in the back yard. We had a yard man who yearly spaded and preuared the soil for planting. We did the weeding and hoeing after that. One didn't have to use a commercial fertilizer in those days. There was plenty of manure available and it had been spread in the late fall all over the garden area — sometimes over the entire yard.

We children helped plant the tiny seeds purchased from the Barteldes Seed Company or the Busch Seed Company.

Our vegetable patch was small. No canning from the garden was done at home, so it was planned for immediate consumption only. We grew green onions, red and white radishes, leaf lettuce, green beans, sometimes a few climbing beans on part of the back fence, a small amount of dill for fall dill pickles, and a little horseradish and parsely. Our eyes still smart thinking back on grinding the horseradish root. We had quite a few rows of leaf lettuce, as wilted lettuce was a favorite at our house. When the radishes came up, it was our task to help thin them out. Radish sandwiches made from fresh lettuce leaves and a layer of radishes on Mr. Henry Gerhardt's or Mr. Planz's rye bread, buttered generously with sweet country butter purchased from Kasold's, were a Sunday night supper treat.

Vegetable gardens eventually thinned out until World War II. Then the Victory gardens were considered a necessity due to food shortages. After that came Company gardens. FMC (formerly Westvaco) donated acreage adjoining the plant for employees who wished to raise vegetables for home use. In other parts of town, several families went together and rented plots of ground.

In planning the early-day flower gardens, the usual list for seeds was nasturtiums, morning glory, hollyhock, and sweet peas. Around Easter time, pansy plants were purchased from Mrs. Paul R. Brooks, whose red brick home and greenhouse on Tennessee Street were where the Theta house now stands. It was closer and more convenient for us to buy most of our plants from Mrs. Whitcomb, whose home and greenhouse stood where the Douglas County State Bank parking lot is. Those living out east and south patronized Mr. Luther whose place was at 15th and Massachusetts on the northwest corner.

Some other popular flowers for the yard were tulips, hyacinths and "flags" (Iris). Roses too, both bushes and climbing, were in most yards. Dorothy Perkins climbers were a favorite before Paul Scarlets came.

There were several large nurseries to supply the trees and shrubs. Adolph Griesa's Mount Hope Nurseries; T. E. Griesa; Ince; and Wm. Frowe were the larger concerns remembered. Mr. Frowe ordered direct from Japan the first Japanese Magnolia trees that were planted in Lawrence. Messrs. Irving Hill, Otto A. Fischer and I. J. Meade, each ordered two of the three-year old trees. That was some 55 years ago. (One at the Fischer residence, 743 Indiana, has survived and is visited every year by many residents. It is now taller than the second story of the house.) The following year an embargo was placed on the magnolias coming into the States and it was a few years before any more could be shipped.

Other old-fashioned shrubs were lilacs, snowballs, spirea, bridal wreath, and Japanese Quince (Japonica).

Going back to vegetable gardens, North Lawrence residents had bigger gardens and many of the negro families made a living from them. Riley Rogers, who at one time was County Treasurer, had one of the largest layouts. He supplied many of the local grocery stores. You drove over to his place if you wanted vegetables for home consumption.

There were other growers who took their products to the residents. They were both men and women. They had regular routes and regular days for delivery. Their wagons usually were one-horse drawn. They would either call out "vegetables," or ring a bell as they came down the street, usually in front of the houses, to let you know they were ready for business.

Housewives would stream out, housedresses, aprons, hair curlers, boudoir caps and all, and usually would have a large tin pan to hold their purchases. Scales were in the wagon. There was no attempt to arrange the vegetables attractively. They were in boxes or bushel baskets. In sweet corn season, the corn was in damp gunny sacks.

There were other things besides vegetables and berries the housewife had peddled to her door. We had milk from the country and not from a creamery. Butter and eggs were brought each Saturday morning from another source. The butter was packed in two-pound, brown jars, (Bennington, no doubt). We can remember back fifty years ago, the price was 25c a pound. During the Depression, fish, chickens, cottage cheese and wild black currants were brought to our back door.

Spring meant other things besides planting. When the elm and maple seeds were falling, we would scoop them up by the handful off of the brick walks and put them in peck baskets. Mr. Barteldes paid up handsomely — 25c a basket. Dandelion and peppergrass digging brought us more spending money from our grandfather Jaedicke.

Spring also meant showers and storms. We were always assured when the severe electrical storms occurred, we need not fear because we had two lightning rods on the roof to prevent being struck. The heavy rains were usually welcome, particularly if we had had a dry spell, as it meant our cisterns would be filled. Nearly every home had at least one cistern and one well. We had two large cisterns and one well because cistern water was piped through the house. The cisterns were covered with a heavy iron lid that had a ring in the center with which to remove it so as to measure the depth of the water. If you couldn't see the water, then one of the men in the family would take a long pole to see how far down the water level was.

For the benefit of the present younger generation, rain water was caught in the guttering and a pipe ran underground into the cistern. Our well had an outside pump. In earlier years, cistern water (soft water), was piped into the kitchen to the dry sink where there was a small hand pump. At Grandmother Fischer's house, the dry sink was hand-made of black walnut and lined in tin. Next to it on a small handmade walnut stand was a bucket of well water. A long-handled tin cup always stayed in the bucket. We did not drink cistern water. The well with a tall pump, was just outside the back door.

In the springtime, Saturdays and Sundays were our fun days. After we had performed our required Saturday chores, we would get on our bicycles and ride either to a woods adjoining the cemetery, or take the Lake View road in the opposite direction. Since there were no paved or black top or gravel roads, it was contingent on how dry the dirt roads were. The woods and country side would be covered with violets, yellow, white and purple, Sweet William, Johnny-Jump-Ups, Jack in the Pulpit, dog tooth violets, and ferns. We would dig up a few plants of each and bring them home to plant in the back yard. Today, that same back yard is covered with the results of those plantings. The Lake View road yielded wild roses, which we never could transplant, primroses, wild strawberries, blackberries and raspberries. Too bad we didn't know about Morel mushrooms then.

If the days were rainy, we'd all assemble in one house and go up to the attic and dig out of the many boxes and trunks, clothes to dress up in. As we grew older, we'd make fudge or divinity or popcorn balls. Then we would take turns reading O'Henry or Dickens out loud while the rest crocheted or embroidered. Those early carefree days were followed by hikes to Lake View via the Santa Fe tracks, some 6 miles or more, and taking the 9 o'clock train back. Others took canoe trips up the Kaw.

Then there were special days. May Day was always observed. You made May baskets of paper and filled them with flowers and hung them on the door knob of your favorite grownup in the block. "Decoration" Day, (Memorial) we would go to the daisy field where the K.U. dormitories now are located at the top of Irving Hill Drive, or on any country road, and pick wild daisies. It was an annual worry in all homes, that rain might destroy the blossoms before Decoration Day.

The day before, in the morning, we would pick most of the blooming flowers in the yard, that would make bouquets for the family graves. Peonies, iris, the old-fashioned red and yellow roses, moss rose, violets and lilacs. When spring came early and warm, then the worry was the flowers might all be gone by Decoration Day. After we cut the flowers, we would sit on the shady, cool back porch and make little bouquets and tie them with string. A large wash tub was filled with several inches of water and the bouquets were placed stems down. Mason fruit jars were assembled by the wash tub.

Early Memorial Day morning, all were packed in the carriage and the family drove to the cemetery. Water was piped near the family lots and we would fill our sprinkling can and fill the glass fruit jars while others placed the bouquets. If we ran out of jars, the flowers were placed on the Myrtle covered graves. Our Grandmother's grave always got one extra bouquet and the prettiest. The other grandmother was still living.

Memorial Day too, meant a preparatory week of visits to the schools by old soldiers, in uniforms, who told us about the Civil War, Spanish American War, and Quantrill's Raid. On that day, each room had a special program with patriotic songs and "pieces" spoken, and ending with a prayer. On Decoration Day there was a parade down Massachusetts Street before the old soldiers went to the cemetery to place flowers and a tiny flag, on the graves of the fallen soldiers.

Those were the days of earthy and simple pleasures.

Printed in Journal-World May 1, 1969

Changing Times and Customs

"TIMES HAVE CHANGED" is heard frequently from old folks. But is it really true?

Take St. Patrick's Day over sixty years ago. You didn't have to be Irish to participate in the activities of that day. Men, women and children, all wore something green to celebrate. It was a green tie, or a green hair ribbon, or a small artificial shamrock pinned on a coat lapel or dress.

April Fool's Day was a day of great sport. Wiedemann's candy store, among others, sold chocolate coated soap in the shape of chocolate caramels and it was great sport to offer a piece to an unsuspecting victim. You called people on the telephone asked them: "Is this 1907?" and when they said you had the wrong number, you would say with glee: "April Fool" and hang up.

Valentine's Day has survived through the years. But the types of valentines have changed. The sentimental old-fashioned kind made with paper lace, and angels or cupids pictured, are missing. The old comic ones are now replaced with the sophisticated contemporary ones. The old comics pictured ugly, distorted faces printed in color on a single sheet of cheap grade paper. Below the face would be some frank, often brutal sentences or verses supposed to apply to the recipient's weaknesses or habits. These sold for a penny. If you got any of these in the mail, you were pretty quiet about it. If they came in the Valentine box in your room at school, usually several youngsters were in on it, so again, it would be hurriedly hidden away from the eyes of your school mates. No one escaped getting at least one funny. Even the teacher got some.

May baskets are getting rare. They were left on the front porch at the door on May Day. The baskets were home made and filled with what garden or wild flowers were in bloom then. You could usually count on violets or dog-tooth violets.

Halloween has improved in the minds of some, for the better. The destruction is not as severe as in years back. Then, outhouses would be turned over, sometimes when occupied. Porch chairs would be found a block or so away on some other porch. Buggies were seen on roof tops, often on a school roof.

When we were real young, we confined out activities to our own block. We were not accompanied by an adult when we made the rounds of each house in the block. There was no trick or treat night. Halloween night was the only night of activity. "Tick Tacks" were our delight. They were made with an empty spool in which notches had been cut, a nail, and some string. The nail was inserted in the hole of the spool. The spool was then placed on the glass of a window and when you pulled the string, it made a startling noise. Screen and storm windows would prohibit that now.

Navy beans were also used on Halloween to throw on porches and against windows. With the price of Navy beans today, one can see mothers discouraging children from using them for play purposes.

Everybody had an autograph album. Our grandmothers had them to. Friends and teachers would write an appropriate verse or sentiment and then sign it. The small book had a hard cover and back, usually with a flower encrusted on the cover in color. "Roses are red, violets are blue, sugar is sweet, and so are you," was one of the popular verses used.

Many social customs have changed. Take for instance, when you walked down the street and spoke to a man or youth, he always tipped his hat. Ladies wouldn't be caught on the street anytime of day without wearing a hat and gloves. If you were in a gathering of men and women, the men always asked permission to smoke. Now the women are likely to out-smoke the men. And men never drank hard liquor in the presence of ladies. Wine was served in a mixed crowd, or beer at a "Dutch lunch" party, but whiskey and gin drinks, never.

When walking along the street with a man escort, he always walked next to the curbing to protect his lady from any potential accident from bolting horses, or splattering of mud and debris on the lady.

Women never applied makeup in public. You retired to the dressing room to freshen up. And you were considered bold and without proper breeding if you crossed your legs when sitting. You wouldn't dare to enter church without a hat and gloves.

Dating a girl years ago meant sitting in the "parlor." After greeting the young man, the family disappeared to some other room in the house.

Does the prospective bridegroom still ask the father for the hand of his daughter?

In the past, a mother-in-law was called, "Mother Jones," and not by her first name. We called the close friends of our parents, "Aunt Mary" and "Uncle Joe," and not by the first name. "Papa'" and "Mama" were universal, as were "Grandma" and "Grandpa." We later graduated to "Father" and "Mother." When we first started using Father and Mother, it was done in a half teasing way to see what the reaction would be. You never heard, Mom, or Pop, or Dad. That would have shown lack of respect for our elders. Many grandparents today want more youthful identification or some nickname.

Beards and long hair worn by young men today reminds one to look at the early-day pictures of the young men that founded Lawrence. In some of the group ones I have viewed, one would think they were a bunch of thugs instead of honest, upright, and well educated citizens. And some of them didn't look too clean either. The long straight hair on the girls today, would have been braided or held back by ribbons. The high updoes look like the pictures of the early 1900's.

In the matter of changes in housekeeping, one day a week was set up for washing — usually Monday. Washing hanging out on a line on a Sunday was regarded as scandalous. Clothes were boiled. Homemade lye soap was used. Irons were heated on the coal or wood stove. If you didn't have a "hired girl" living in, you had a "washwoman" come to the house. Clothes were scrubbed on a wash board. Sometimes you had the washing done out by a washwoman and you didn't pay by the pound, but by the size of the washbasket.

We had butter delivered to us once a week, by a lady living in the country, (that location now in the city limits and heavily populated). It was put in brown Bennington jars that held two pounds of butter. We took at least two jars a week, and more at Christmas when there was more baking. Bakery bread was a treat and luxury in our house. Henry Gerhardt's bakery rye bread or Plantz's, was a special treat.

Ice was delivered by wagon. We had an ice-box that held 100 pounds. Every house had an ice card. It was of square cardboard about twelve inches square, and on each side was a number, either 25-50-75-100, in large lettering. When you needed ice, you placed the card in the kitchen window facing the alley. If you thought you needed 25 pounds, the 25 side of the card would face to the top. If you couldn't figure how much you needed, you put the back side out and the ice man would come in and decide for you.

The ice wagon was pulled by horses. On hot summer days, the children in the neighborhood would follow the wagon down the alley and beg for ice chips. You knew when the ice man was coming, because he would start in the alley shouting: "Ice — Ice," to give the housewife time to hang up her card. In later years, many a KU football player worked for the ice company and would carry in those heavy cakes of ice on his back. A large dish pan was placed under the ice box for the water from the melted ice to drip into. On hot days, it had to be emptied several times a day. Many a housewife would forget and come into her kitchen or pantry to find water all over the floor. Some people kept an ice box on the back porch and often boys thought it a great prank to rob the ice boxes for food.

In the days before stainless steel, kitchen knives would get stained. A Saturday morning chore for us was to rub the steel blades with a piece of soft brick to make them nice and shiney.

When telephones came into existence, the operator was always called, "Central." She would be deluged with calls when the fire bell rang to know where the fire was. And she always gave you the information. If you asked for a number and she informed you it was busy, you would ask to have her call you when they were through talking and she would obligingly call you.

Can you imagine a hamburger today at a stand, thick enough for you to order it "rare," or 'well done?" They were just 5 and 10 cents, according to sizes.

Dancing was never like it is today. No dancing by yourself. The closer your partner held you, especially for the dreamy waltzes, the better you liked it—cheek to cheek even! The music had to be melodious to be popular. The "orchestra" instead of the "band" always ended the last dance of the evening by playing "Good Night Ladies." And everybody walked home.

Printed in Journal-World February 5, 1969

Trains

TRAINS! JUST THE MERE WORD conjures up myriad happy recollections. To the young, trains were fascinating, exciting, and romantic. Who doesn't recall the many times he has watched a train pull into a station and looked in the windows at the passengers peering out and wondered where to and why that train was carrying them? Or in the night, you have heard the train whistles and wished you were there riding to some exciting, unknown destination. Those early train whistles had a different tone—more melodious—not the shrill sound of those in the mountains that echoed back and forth in the canyons and not the mournful whoo-whoo of the present ones.

And those who have worked for a railroad remember the togetherness in the profession. The railroad family is a close-knit, loyal family. No matter what system or line you worked for, you belonged in the "family". They are solid people.

In Lawrence, one of the Sunday events for children to look forward to, was for grandparents or parents to take them to the station to see the trains come thundering in. The engineer always waved as did many of the passengers. Those early huge engines, fueled by soft coal, spewed out black smoke and soot.

Sometimes the train would stop below the station to take on water from the water tank. Sometimes, if it was a through train, the station agent would come out and flag the train to stop and take on a traveler going beyond Topeka or Kansas City. The engineer would toot to indicate he got the signal. Sometimes the station agent had a message attached to a long hooped stick and the engineer would reach out and take it off as he went by.

Occasionally the through train would slow down just slow enough to enable a man to hop off. This would most likely be a Smithmeyer, Kirchoff or Barteldes. They were big shippers and they would have been to Kansas City or Topeka on business. If the train came to a full stop, the bell on the engine had to keep ringing until the train pulled out. You might be able to see the fireman shoveling coal in the boiler and you'd watch the hot, red and orange coals lick up the black coal. Then the brakeman, and the conductor would call, "All aboard!" and in too short a time the train would slowly pull out.

On most through trains, there was an observation platform on the last coach and maybe there would be a celebrity or political figure standing against the brass rail and shaking hands with some of the town's spectators. Other travelers might be sitting on camp-stool chairs. Often at night, passengers took advantage of being able to get a little fresh air.

Another fascinating place was the inside of the station. Benches and brass cuspidors, more commonly known in those days as spittoons, were the main furnishings in the waiting room. At the ticket agent's counter, the telegraph keys would be ticking away and you wished you knew the Morse code to decipher it, always imagining perhaps there might have been a train robbery or wreck and the news was just coming in. There was a wall telephone and the agent rang his party by turning a black-handled crank. Off of the waiting room was the baggage room and at the Santa Fe station, Mr. K. C. Evans was in command. Trunks, suit cases, express packages, and many other articles would be piled high. Mr. Evans was never too busy to exchange a few words with you.

Station agents in the early years were, John Robinson and before him, J. T. Shanklin, at the Union Pacific; and at the Santa Fe, Geo. C. Bailey and later W. W. Burnett, then E. P. Addy.

At one time, Lawrence was serviced by three railroad lines and there was a train to Kansas City almost every hour, and the same to return. The Santa Fe, in south Lawrence, had its "Plug". It was a "milk train", local, and stopped at every station from Lawrence to Kansas City. It probably was called the "Plug" because it plugged along. There was a branch line, south, that high school teams and fans took to Ottawa for football games.

The Union Pacific in North Lawrence had important through-traffic and a branch that went to Tonganoxie and Leavenworth.

The Rock Island used the Union Pacific tracks from Kansas City to Topeka and there were certain restrictions to passenger service. You had to be traveling west beyond Topeka and east beyond Kansas City to be able to board it at Lawrence.

In those days, about the only means of travel was by train. Passenger travel was heavy with students and vacationers. The trains were very long, consisting of chair cars, diners, pullman coaches and sometimes five or six baggage cars.

When we started out on a trip, we went to the station in a hack eitheir from Donnelly's or Moak's livery stable. Usually several hours earlier, our trunk and extra suitcases were taken to the station in a horse-drawn express wagon, to be checked and ready to be loaded on the train. Often we boarded the Pullman at night on the Santa Fe for Colorado Springs.

There were times to be remembered of violent wind storms, the roof of the paper mill being blown off and landing on the tracks, all communication wires down, and passengers stranded on the train until the tracks could be cleared.

These were the times before bedroom or roomettes. You either traveled Pullman or chair car. The Pullman seats were called "sections" and you had an upper and a lower berth for sleeping. They did have drawing rooms and compartments at the end of the Pullman coach, but in early times they were not generally patronized due to being more expensive. When it came time for bed, we undressed in the ladies lounge at the end of the coach, while the porter made up our beds. A heavy green curtain hung down to cover both upper and lower berths. Each berth had a small green hammock strung across the windows for smaller articles of wearing apparel. Mother would put her watch and extra money, and rings, in a little chamois bag hung around her neck by a fine cord. In daytime, the chamois was firmly pinned to her corset. She kept her Elk pin on her dress. She always wore something to show she was the wife of an Elk or a Knights Templar. This was insurance for extra protection or service in case of an unforeseen emergency.

A child's observation showed most conductors wore a Masonic emblem or Elk's tooth, or both, attached to their watch chain.

Riding along in the night, you might be awakened by the train coming to a stop after much jerking and grinding of brakes. You would raise your window curtain to see the brakeman swinging his lighted lantern as he walked along. Or many times in the summer, as the train crept along slowly, stopping now and then, you could see water close up to the tracks and the conductor would tell you the next morning there had been a washout and the train would be several hours late. Sometimes a trainman would be seen climbing a telegraph pole to send a message. Or perhaps you would see a passenger being greeted at a lonely station platform by one person.

To get up or down the upper berth, you rang for the porter. He brought a ladder and while the train rocked and swayed, he'd steady you until you tumbled in. As the trains in summer time particularly, were sooty and dusty, the women wore dust caps to bed to keep their hair clean. They were crocheted or made of some fine cotton material.

Life on the train was full of excitement. As we sped over the prairies, we'd play a game of counting prairie dogs before they ducked down in their mounds, or watch coyotes loping for miles across the flat, hot, sandy land. The porter was always our best companion. He would play games with us. A train butcher broke the monotony by walking through many times during the day hawking his wares of fruit, candy, magazines and newspapers. We would stop the conductor to ask him if the train was running on time and he would solemnly pull out his gold pocket watch and give us the information and perhaps sit down and visit with us.

Another pastime was to watch through the window to see the engine and cars winding along through a canyon and then look back to see the end of our train. It would take two engines to pull the long trains when we started to climb into higher altitude. The extra one was added somewhere along the way.

Everybody was friendly. You became acquainted with every passenger in your coach, without exception. Passengers would walk down the aisle and stop and exchange pleasantries. The children would play together. Before you got off, you knew everybody's name, where they were from, and their destination. If the train was going to do some switching, the conductor would inform everybody ahead of time and the passengers would get off and stretch and perhaps go into the station for a cup of coffee.

Some trains carried diners. In the morning and before each meal, a waiter walked through the train calling loudly, "First call for breakfast in the dining car" and at the end of serving time, "Last call for breakfast in the dining car". The road bed was rough at times and you'd stagger to your table as the dining car swayed and bumped. It was not unusual to see your dishes slide to the edge of the table or liquids spill all over the table cloth. But that was part of the fun.

Most often, the lunch meal was eaten in our seat. A shoe box holding fried chicken among other goodies, had been prepared at home before we started.

The Santa Fe carried no diners on the Colorado trains because there were "Harvey Houses" at strategic points along the route. Dodge City was one of them. They were famous for the quality of the food and the impecable service. The conductor came through the train to find out how many passengers were going to eat in the dining room and would then wire ahead the number. There was also a lunch room and counter at the stations, also run by Harvey. We generally ate there. As the train pulled into the station, you were greeted by a man standing on the platform beating on a huge brass gong. This ritual was performed at all Harvey stations at meal time.

As the train neared our destination, one at a time, we would stand in the aisle and the porter brushed us off for any traces of dust, starting at your shoulders and going all the way, front and back, including your shoes. The men got their hats brushed also. Goodbyes were exchanged and you stepped off the train eagerly looking forward to more exciting adventures in the mountains.

Printed in Journal-World Dec. 16, 1970

Robinson Gymnasium

MANY BEAUTIFUL VIEWS COULD BE SEEN from the windows of old Robinson gymnasium and from the top of the fire escape, when it was completed in 1907. From the south side, the view swept over the Wakarusa Valley to the south, and beyond to the Pleasant Grove hill, with nothing to break it but farmland. To the southeast, was Haskell Institute, and beyond that Blue Mound, and to the west, the Daisy Field. The view from the north windows took in the town of Lawrence, the Kaw river, and the valley stretching for ten miles to the hills.

The view now is perhaps not so inspiring, but just as breathtaking, because of the changes in the scenery. The farmland is now filled by almost solid apartment buildings and homes, and dotted by business and motel signs. The trees are so tall and thick to the southeast, you can barely make out Haskell. Blue Mound shows signs of a ski lift and run. Stouffer Place apartments and the giant dormitories have filled up the Daisy Field to the west. Strong Hall and trees have shut out the view on the north entirely.

Old Robinson soon will be torn down to make room for a new humanities building, Wescoe Hall.

Many strange sights and events have taken place during the lifetime of Robinson Gymnasium. It has seen co-eds taking boxing lessons from the "Fightin' Parson", Earl Blackman. To be sure there were only three girls taking, but one today boasts she taught her three sons the fundamentals, and the lessons came in handy. It has seen several baptismal ceremonies conducted in the pool.

Many famous people graced its halls. Billy Sunday, the famous evangelist, sang, "Brighten the Corner Where You Are", and the students joined in, at a convocation. William Jennings Bryan gave a commencement address there. It can boast of entertaining a president of the United States.

Under the auspices of the University Y. M. C. A., William Howard Taft opened the chapel exercises at the beginning of the fall semester in 1911. John Philip Sousa and his band played there — Madame Schumnn-Heink sang there; Efrem Zimbalist gave a violin concert; the Minneapolis Symphony Orchestra of fifty performers, and the Lawrence Ladies Chorus of sixteen solo voices, performed there. A centennial anniversary of the birth of Abraham Lincoln took place there in 1909.

It has watched women's gym clothes change from middy blouses and bloomers and long stockings, to T-shirts and shorts and socks.

Old Robinson years ago began to show its age. Like an old bearded man, it became almost completely covered with trumpet vine and ivy that turned a brilliant red in the fall. It became difficult even to see that the building was faced with Oread lime-stone. Bird nests were all over the place. Even owls nested there every year. In early spring, on the east side, you could see the baby owls sticking their heads out over the nest and later clinging to the top ledge. When you walked up the front steps, the stones were so worn by countless feet, your shoes almost fit in a groove. The walls inside were discolored and damp, especially after heavy rainstorms.

Some changes inside were made over the years. The women's dressing room, originally had wooden cubicles where at that time, you were too modest to undress or dress around anyone. These cubicles were so small, you backed in and by all sorts of contor-tions, you managed to get in and out of your gym clothes. You had more things to take off in those days.

Later there was one long room with benches on the sides to sit on and lockers to store your things. The pool was made longer from fifty feet to sixty feet. The original depth was eight or nine feet all over, but later the depth was graduated. Originally, beginners had no shallow water to stand in, you either swam or else. It is said, that was the theory of Dr. James Naismith. The gym was divided for the men and women by sliding, accordian type doors, and they always had trouble closing them. Now a permanent partition has been installed.

Robinson Gymnasium can claim it had more activities than any other building on the campus ever had or ever will have. As soon as the building was completed, every student attending K. U. had to start at Robinson for registration and enrollment. To get a degree, one of the requirements was that you had completed two years of physical training, and could swim the length of the fifty-foot pool, or at least try.

All physical examinations for both men and women were given there for years, and only by Dr. Naismith. All basketball games were played there. State high school basketball tourna-ments were held there for both boys and girls.

In the days before the dormitories were built, the visiting boys and girls often slept on cots in the building. When service men and women returned after World War II, the two floors had bunks for men students who couldn't find suitable housing. For the early relays and band festivals, cots were placed on both floors to accommodate the participating students and their equip-ment.

All fine arts programs took place there. The opening exer-cises of the University were held in the "Auditorium". In the early years, commencement exercises as well as the commence-ment dinners, were held there. The exercises were in the morning, on the second floor. Folding chairs were set up and bleacher seats were installed around the running track in the balcony. A stage was built at one end of the room for the speakers. After the exercises, the commencement dinner followed at noon in the gymnasium on the first floor. Mr. R. B. Wagstaff catered these dinners for many years. The meal was prepared and cooked by the top cateress for Lawrence society matrons, Mrs. Lucy Brown. The dinner was served by Lawrence High School girls—juniors and seniors. It was considered quite an honor to be invited to serve, without pay. Church auxiliaries also prepared and served several of these dinners.

For years, Mr. T. J. Sweeney, Sr., a former student, furnished cape jasmines for the dinner, and there was one at each place on the long tables that filled the gymnasium. Down the middle of the tables were bouquets of wild daisies, picked at the Daisy field by some of the high school girls who served. Sometimes daisy chains trailed on each side of the bouquets. The kitchen, where the meal was prepared on three big ranges, was in the southeast corner of the first floor. Later that room had an upright piano, a chair, and a small table, and the north wall was mirrored. It later served girls taking dancing lessons.

October 6, 1911, Woman's Day was celebrated to "inaugurate a state wide movement for the building for University girls", under the auspices of the Alumni Association of the University. After the program in which all of the speeches were made by women only, luncheon was served in the gymnasium, followed by an automobile ride for those who wanted it. The only man participating in the program was Chancellor Strong, who conducted the devotional exercises. The following April, 1912, an Indoor Circus was given by the Department of Physical Education for the benefit of the women's dormitory fund.

In 1916, April 10, the first transcontinental telephone K. U. Alumni reunion was held in the gym. Five hundred persons, including faculty, alumni, and a few students listened by individual earphones, to speakers in San Francisco, New York and Lawrence. And in 1922, the first "radio rally" was staged in Robinson. December 15, 1924, the dedicatory program of KFKU went out on radio and the listening audience heard it from Robinson Gym.

Major campus social events were held in Robinson, including the sophomore hop and the junior prom. All of these were preceded by a dinner on the first floor, followed by the grand march and dancing on the second. Even the "Junior Farce" put on by the junior class of 1913, a one-act musical farce, was performed there.

The Gymnasium was patterned after the Springfield, Massachusetts Y.M.C.A. Training School, where Dr. Naismith came from. It was on his recommendation that the balcony was constructed as a running track. It was one of the few gymnasiums on a college campus of this size that housed activities of both men and women in the same building.

Every department of physical education was housed there before Allen Field House was built. The Traffic Offices were there at one time. The Athletic office was used to display the trophies. Then in 1917, more room was needed, so they were stored. In 1932, the trophy case, given by the graduating class of 1928, was installed in the Student Union and loving cups and silver plaques have been on display there ever since.

Robinson Gymnasium served its University well. It served Uncle Sam too. Part of the Machinist Mates program during World War II, was carried on there, as well as the Navy V-12; Navy V-5 Flight Training, and the Army Student Training Program, (ASTP).

The old gymnasium didn't go uncriticized, despite its many services rendered. In 1914, the Yellow Kansan, (but printed on pink paper), stated, "Kansas Fire Laws Flouted in Robinson Auditorium", Students Lives Menaced by Lack of Escape. Barred Windows and Too Many Seats Between Aisles. Gym Not Fireproof", "Billions of Bacteria Menace Swimmers in Waters of Gym Pool". These were the headlines, but the article following, backed down by saying, "Bacteria not sufficiently numerous to cause any alarm".

Old Robinson soon will go the way of most old and outmoded public buildings, but it will be missed by many people who have fond memories of the place.

Journal-World Annual University of Kansas Edition—1965.

The Campus on Mount Oread

WHEN YOU LOOK AT THE lush, sophisticated, well-groomed University of Kansas campus today, it is difficult to realize that back in 1866, it was completely barren. In fact, there were no buildings or trees or shrubs on either North College Hill, or what is now our present campus. It was just a hilly pasture with a few scattered, wooden fences bordering small plots of pasture land, and no trees.

Today, the campus offers many inviting spots to entice students, faculty, alumni, and visitors. To name a few: the Green east of Fraser, the Stadium area, Marvin Grove, Potter Lake and the picnic grounds on the west hill, Fowler Grove and the wide sloping spread of green below the Campanile, which used to be part of the old Oread Golf course.

As the University grew, more land was acquired, and that made these beautiful spots possible. For many years, the Green to the east of Fraser was used for rallys and accompanying bonfires, May Day fights, and May pole dances, senior class dances around the totem pole, class breakfasts and smoking of the peace pipes. K.U.'s first Christmas tree program took place around a big pine tree just north of Blake Hall. The tree was electrically lighted and carols were sung. Money had been raised for Christmas relief in 1920, and the following year for relief of European students.

After Chancellor Marvin had been chancellor three years, he decided it was time to beautify the campus. When he came to the University, the grounds were still bare. He had a friend and admirer in Joseph Savage, a farmer living south of the Hill. His daughter was attending K. U. Mr. Savage got tired looking up toward the University and seeing such barrenness. He offered Chancellor Marvin some trees and shrubs if he would see that they were properly planted and taken care of.

And so, on Arbor Day, 1878, Mr. Savage brought lilac cions from his own yard that he had cut and rooted, and a wagon load of small trees dug up from along the Wakarusa River. Some of these were redbud, and Mr. Marvin personally planted one to the south of Dyche Museum. Volunteer students helped prepare the ground. It was an all-day affair and girls furnished a picnic lunch for the workers. The result: the beautiful lilac hedge along Lilac Lane, and the beginning of Marvin Grove.

Sometime later, the Douglas County Horticultural Society set out more trees, and a stone retaining wall was placed along the south side of 14th Street. A gate was placed there and this kept stray cattle off of the grounds.

Marvin Grove winds down back of Strong and Bailey Halls. Originally a narrow, rocky path ran to the east, and a little brook bordered it. The path was called "Lover's Lane". In the 1920's, the Grove was used for the May Day Fetes.

At one time a nine-hole golf course skirted Marvin Grove. In the summer of 1899, several professors attempted to stimulate interest in a golf course. It took all summer to get things started, but they finally achieved a membership of fifty, including towns people. There is no record of any student getting hit by a stray golf ball, but the course was not kept up well and finally was abandoned not long after the Lawrence Country Club was organized.

McCook Field was to the north and west of Marvin Grove. In the beginning, athletic events such as football and baseball, took place on a privately owned field at the corner of 14th Street and Massachusetts, where the present Junior High School stands. Whenever games were played, the owner of the field collected a percentage of the receipts. The location was too far away from the campus for practices and the Athletic Association decided it was time to purchase land for a field closer to the University.

School authorities were interested in a pasture and farm land north and west of Marvin Grove. Part of that land was owned by ex-Governor Charles Robinson. He gave half of the pasture to the University and Dr. John J. McCook, who had a degree of L.L.D. from KU in 1890, gave $1,500 toward the purchase of more land, and later doubled the amount.

The field was laid out to run east and west. A grandstand was built in the northeast corner. Benches were set out and later bleacher seats were built on the north and south side of the field. At first, many of the fans from town, came with horse and buggy, and the buggies were lined up on one side of the field, but the people stood in front to watch the games. The horses were unharnessed and tied near the Grove. Automobiles soon took the place of buggies, and they were lined up in front of the bleachers and the occupants often sat on the back seats of their cars.

Track and Relays followed. May 6, 1911, the 8th Annual Interscholastic Track and Field Meet was held at McCook Field. Some of the officials were: Dr. Joseph A. Reilley, referee; Dr. James Naismith, starter; Prof. C. B. Root, scorer; Ralph Spotts (a Lawrence student) was the announcer. It took a booming voice in those days—no loud speakers, only a megaphone.

When World War I came along, the land bordering McCook to the east, just off of Mississippi Street, took on a military air. In 1918, barracks were erected for the Student Army Training Corps of some 2500 men. It was a familiar sound to all residents of west Lawrence to hear the bugle calls for reveille, drill and taps.

Following the war, many changes occurred on the campus. A drive was launched to construct a memorial for those who had died during the War. Funds were raised to construct a stadium and a student union building as a memorial. It was decided to build the stadium on McCook Field. The old stands were demolished by students and faculty on Stadium Day, May 10, 1921.

To the east of McCook, Commencement exercises were held under a huge tent in 1923. This did not work out so well, it was too hot and that idea for future commencements was abolished.

Fowler Grove seems pretty small to be called a "grove", but next to McCook Field, it probably was used by more people than any other spot on the campus. It lies in front of the Journalism building, formerly the Fowler Shops, and just east of Robinson Gymnasium. For many years, alumni, seniors and faculty, gathered there for the march to Robinson Gymnasium, and later at the temporary wooden Union, for commencement day dinners.

When the summer recreation program was started in the 1930's, Fowler Grove became and still is, the center for the outdoor play equipment and games in the evenings. It was started by Dr. Forrest Allen in connection with the Physical Education Community Recreation classes in Summer School, and was supervised by them. After World War II, it was used as a means of giving the Elementary School Physical Education classes practical experience. They planned and supervised the program while Summer School was in session, and in turn staff members supervised them. Open to the public, it probably was the only recreation center in the country situated in the heart of a big university campus.

Potter Lake was "built" primarily to provide extra water for the University in case of fire. There was a natural hollow already there, so it seemed to be the logical place for a lake. Excavation was completed by March, 1911. T. M. Potter, a former member of the Board of Regents, and then a state senator, was given the honor of having the lake named after him. At one time, boating, regattas, and swimming all took place there. A sand beach, diving board, and dressing tents were installed. Several unfortunate drownings, brought the authorities to the decision to ban all water activities there.

Ice skating in winter continues to be popular. Small boys can often be seen fishing and frog catching all the year round. The familiar sight at any of these inviting spots, in years past, was to see couples strolling along the paths or studying under the trees, or picnicking. Now, another element has been added—small tots (future Jayhawkers), are seen playing, or sleeping on a blanket, while the parents are studying, or just plain resting.

The picnic grounds given by the Class of 1943, and completed in 1946, are situated on the western slope from Potter Lake, and afford a beautiful, restful view. They serve many people and in the seasons for picnics and it is not uncommon to see dancing on the cement floor.

Chancellor Marvin started the drive to beautify the campus. Chancellor Lindley saw that trees were planted on both sides of Jayhawk Boulevard, but it took Chancellor Malott, with an efficient Buildings and Grounds organization, to go all out to beautify the entire campus. Mrs. Deane Malott and Mrs. John Nelson advised on the placing of the flowering trees and shrubs.

Several graduating classes made their class gift to the University as a gift of landscaping certain spots with plants and trees. There are markers dotting the campus showing where plantings were made in memory of friends and former students of the University. The streets throughout the campus were given permanent names. Chancellor Franklin Murphy followed by encouraging gifts for the campus.

The Chi Omega fountain was installed. Several loyal, generous alumni made it possible to have the grounds at the Museum of Art landscaped and statuary placed there. Chancellor Wescoe continued to display the same interest, and as a result, the University of Kansas campus is one of the most beautiful and talked about campuses in the world.

Printed in Journal-World—Annual Univ. of Kansas Edition—Fall of 1965.

North Lawrence And Bismarck Grove

NORTH LAWRENCE, where the Westvaco Plant (FMC now) is located, has an early history all its own. Bismarck Grove, which is in North Lawrence and across the Union Pacific tracks directly north of FMC's operations, now a grove of old trees and a few buildings, was once one of the most colorful spots in eastern Kansas.

The site of North Lawrence (the Kaw River separates North Lawrence from South Lawrence) was part of the land reserved for the Delaware Indians by a treaty dated September 24, 1829. From that time until 1854 these lands were in the Indian Country or Nebraska Territory.

In 1860, in a treaty between the United States and the Delaware Indians, the Government granted to Sarcoxie, chief of the Turtle Band, approximately 320 acres which included a greater part of North Lawrence. A year later, all of this land was transferred by Sarcoxie and his wife to three early settlers, Charles Robinson, Robert Stevens, and Wm. A. Simpson. Shortly afterwards, the tract was broken up by the transfer of a strip of land to the Eastern Division of the Kansas Pacific Railroad Company and other smaller pieces to settlers who moved to the community. In the following two years, quite a bit of building went on in North Lawrence, with churches, houses, schools, a post office, a newspaper, a jail, stores, and a hotel called "Crandall House."

Back in 1854 when the early settlers located on the south banks of the Kaw River, there was little vegetation or timber, but the north side had a dense growth. So many people crossed the river to obtain materials to erect their buildings and homes.

On September 20, 1863, the telegraph line of the Kansas Pacific Railroad was completed to North Lawrence. Kansas Pacific began laying its line from Wyandotte (Kansas City, Kansas) to North Lawrence during '63 and it was completed November, 1864. Regular train service began a month later.

Citizens of South Lawrence were ambitious to have Lawrence the county seat of Douglas County, therefore, they wanted to bring in North Lawrence. So in 1865 the Legislature provided for the formation of Grant Township which borders North Lawrence on the east and north and made it a part of Douglas County instead of Jefferson County. Later Lawrence got to be the county seat of Douglas County.

At the edge of the city limits of North Lawrence, directly across the Union Pacific tracks north of the Westvaco plant, is Bismarck Grove, at one time one of the most colorful spots in eastern Kansas. Where the name Bismarck originated is a matter of conjecture. A herd of buffalo was kept in the grove at one time and the leader of the herd was called Bismarck. The buffalo is the symbol of the Union Pacific Railroad. It is hard to tell if the grove was named for the buffalo or the buffalo named for the grove. Too, having been a beer garden originally, it might have been named by German residents after the famous German general. The grove later became the location for the shops of the Kansas Pacific Railroad (now Union Pacific).

The Grove's best years were in the 1880's and 1890's. When the Union Pacific and Kansas Pacific were consolidated in 1880, the new company made extensive improvements, and many buildings were erected. State and county fairs sponsored by the Union Pacific and directed by the Western National Fair Association were held. At that time the Grove contained about 100 acres, 40 of which were heavily timbered with large oaks, elms, and walnuts. A lake was made and stocked with swans to give it an elegant appearance.

About this time a prominent song writer and publisher by the name of Leslie was conducting vocal classes in all the surrounding towns. In 1879 the graduates of these classes were brought together at Bismarck Grove under the name of Leslie Choral Union. The pavilion or tabernacle built to accommodate 2,000 singers and 3,000 spectators was too small to hold between 10,000 and 12,000 visitors who had arrived from all over the state to hear them. Railroad facilities were taxed to the utmost and a part of the crowd came on flat cars fitted with seats and no roof overhead. This gave many people of Kansas their first introduction to Bismarck Grove which later became the site for the fairs.

There were many colorful goings-on in the Grove for 10 years, and it was well advertised in many newspapers. To attract more people, the mule car line was extended from South Lawrence to the Grove. Fare was five cents. When the car made the turn at the north end of the bridge, it invariably went off the tracks; the men patrons would all climb out and help lift it back again.

When patrons arrived at the Grove, they saw swans swimming around the lake at the entranceway, everybody in their best bib and tucker, carriages arriving drawn by spirited horses, and the entire family attending. There were many buildings such as Machinery Hall, Fine Arts Gallery, Carriage Shed, Exhibition Building, Telegraph Office, Reporter's Cottage, Director's Office, Grandstand, Judges' Stand, stables to house 500 horses, cattle stalls, and hog and sheep pens, all with the ginger-bread trimmings of those times.

Walks and fountains graced the entire area, all shaded by lovely trees. The exhibits were displayed like the fairs of today.

Horse racing was a big feature. The Grove had the fastest mile trotting track west of the Allegheny Mountains. There were relays for girl riders each year, one team was a Lawrence team and the other from Missouri. Feeling ran so high that finally this race had to be discontinued. Possibly it was a carryover from the early turbulent days in Lawrence.

Toward the close of the 1890's the fairs became more local and due to the depression, they were finally discontinued in 1898. The Grove was then used by Captain Wm. S. Tough as a depot for congregating Shetland ponies to be shipped for the Boer War to South Africa—15,000 head were shipped during that time. The herd of Shetlands was originally imported from the Shetland Islands and was headed by the celebrated stallion, Buck Stop. Diaz, one-time President of Mexico, had three ponies from this herd in his private stables.

In 1903 and again in 1951, the disastrous flood waters of the Kaw River surged into the Grove. Today, when you drive across the cattle guard at the gate, the loud clatter resounds, disturbing the peaceful quietness of the area. You find yourself surrounded by fine old shade trees including one elm and one oak that measure the largest on record in Kansas. You have to drive up to the fine modern house made from the ticket seller's building, before you can see the lake with its deep banks. And the tabernacle is now being used to store feed as Bismarck Grove today is being used as a feeding station, now for beef mostly, and a few sheep.

Visitors come away with the feeling that all the buildings may eventually be destroyed by fire or flood or age, but the trees and the Grove are there to stay.

Published in Westvaco Digest — September 1952.

Lawrence's Only and Oldest Team Whist Club

ALONG WITH ALL ITS CULTURAL ASPECTS, Lawrence has also been known for its many card-playing clubs. It is doubtful if any of the original ones have survived as long as the Monday Team Whist Club. It is well over sixty-five years old.

To begin with, team whist is unique. It is a highly competitive game. It is played with duplicate boards, but all hands are held up. You rely on memory, legitimate inferential signals from your partner, and your opponents, to take as many tricks as you can with your thirteen-card hand. In Team Whist, the scoring is done the opposite way you score for duplicate bridge. The winning team that has the fewest losses, rather than the highest score, is the winner.

The Monday Team Whist Club was organized sometime around the turn of the century. It was then called the Monday Whist Club and straight whist was played, as duplicate had not been taken up yet. In 1904, the members decided to make a duplicate game of it, and they called themselves, "The Monday Team Whist Club". As far as can be determined from the records, its original members were: Mrs. Floyd Doubleday; Mrs. Loren Wilson; Mrs. J. T. Shanklin (mother of Mrs. A. J. Boynton); Mrs. Serenity Morrison; Mrs. Frank Anderson; Mrs. James Green, (wife of "Uncle Jimmy" Green, former Dean of the Law School); Mrs. Sol Marks, (mother of Julius Marks); Mrs. W. D. Brownell; Mrs. Peter Emery; Mrs. F. H. Smithmeyer, (grandmother of Fred C. Smithmeyer); Mrs. R. C. Morrow, (mother of Mrs. T. J. Sweeney); and Mrs. M. G. Manley, (mother-in-law of Mrs. Robert C. Manley).

The members were very "choosy" about their substitutes. They would invite them to substitute for the current year only, so that if they didn't like the way they played, or they didn't seem to fit in, they were not invited to participate the next year.

Whist is the popular social card game that dates as far back as before 1700. Edmond Hoyle wrote a short treatise on the game of whist in 1742. (Playing cards date back to 1440). Auction bridge and contract bridge came much later. Whist derived its name from the exclamation, "Hist" and "Whisk", meaning to pay attention, and to be silent. And the Monday Team Whist Club today, still tries to maintain and do just that. When some of the older players were still playing, if a player talked too loud, or made too much noise, a knock on the table would silence her immediately. In the old days there was no conversation during the play.

Mrs. E. E. Bayles recalls coming home from school when the club was in session, and tiptoeing upstairs to her room. Today, when the players get settled down, sometimes the silence is only broken by the snapping of the cards, as they are played on the table.

One of the stories passed down by an older member, was that the club met on Mondays, (the traditional wash day), so that everybody would know those members did not do their own washing.

Mrs. Robert C. Manley, a former member, gave these wise words of advice to a new member: "Don't play too fast; quiet; don't talk over the hands; try to put your Bridge rules out of your mind; leads and discards have to be watched, as you do not have the advantage of seeing the exposed hand, that you do in Bridge."

Traditions in the Monday Team Whist Club have been carefully guarded. Playing starts every Monday promptly at 2:00 p.m. Fines were imposed in the old days if someone was late, but this has not been carried on. Twenty-five boards are played in an afternoon. When fifteen have been played, tea time is announced. Refreshments are secondary in the club—the game comes first. Refreshments consist of "one wet and one dry", but they have digressed somewhat on this. Tea and coffee are both offered, a rich dessert, and nuts or candy.

The partner of the hostess always pours. Scores are read outloud, identified by the team number and not by the players' names, during the refreshment break, and again at the completion of the 25 boards. The director of the boards and the game, Mrs. E. E. Bayles, (and her job goes on from year to year), designates who the players team up with. Since the beginning of the club, individual scores are kept on each player, (and records date back to 1904), for eleven meetings. This way, each player gets to play with each member sometime in those eleven times. There are no prizes, as the honor of winning is all the players seem to care about.

The secretary's reports were the usual type, except in 1921, when this bit of whimsy was added: "April 3 — Mrs. Banks — A rainy day — the apricot tree in full bloom, but we'll never see it again. It blew down April eighth."

The secretary's other duty is to call the substitutes if they are needed. The hostess for the next meeting takes the duplicate boards and supplies, (kept in a suit case), home with her and prepares the hands for the next meeting. The cards are dealt out and the last card dealt is the trump suit for that board, and so designated on the score sheet.

Another tradition that is carefully kept, is that a member who is not physically able to continue playing in the club, still remains a member unless she sends a note of resignation. Her place for play is filled by a substitute. Initiation fees and dues have increased in the last sixty-five years, but they are still modest. They are used for supplies and flowers. But here again, flowers are only sent if members of an immediate family are involved. Through the years, special assessments were made to contribute to some worthy cause, such as Relief Fund; Christmas boxes; Red Cross and Community Chest.

Today, the present members are: Mrs. Frank Stockton; Mrs. T. D. Funk; Mrs. Worthy Horr; Mrs. E. E. Bayles; Mrs. Will Pendleton; Miss Agnes Thompson; Mrs. Laurence Woodruff; Mrs. W. R. Banker; Mrs. M. F. Hudson; Mrs. Wm. Paden; Mrs. A. T. Walker; Mrs. Fay Brown. Some of the ladies who substitute frequently are: Mrs. Ruth Skinner; Mrs. A. B. Mitchell; Mrs. A. C. Lonborg; and Mrs. Frank Scanlan. The present officers are: Mrs. E. E. Bayles, president, and Mrs. Will Pendleton, secretary.

Due to the complexity of the game, the club sometimes is hard put for substitutes. However, substitutes are given typed rules to study and usually some of the members arrange an evening or two of play, so as to explain some of the leads and signals. The determination of the dedicated members to keep the club together, along with the enthusiasm of the substitutes, overcomes all obstacles and keeps the club strong.

Printed in Journal-World Feb. 12, 1966

KU Freshmen 50 Years Ago

WHEN K. U. STARTED ON ITS second century this fall (1966), the new freshmen looked decidedly different from those fifty years before. Then, the Lawrence freshman woman bought her clothes from Innes, Bullene & Hackman; Newmark's, or Weaver's. There were no specialty shops. Today, the colorful array of sweaters and skirts and blouses might be purchased in Lawrence, Topeka or Kansas City. Sweaters were worn, but they were not the lovely cashmeres of today. They were thick and bulky and dark, and were worn in place of a jacket. Mini-skirts? The skirts then were ankle length, covering long, black, lisle stockings and high top shoes. The shoes would have been purchased at Fischer's Shoe Store or Starkweather's.

The girls wore their long hair combed fairly high, sort of a modified pompadour effect. Some ratting (now called "teasing"), was necessary to achieve best results. Makeup? You would have been considered "Fast", if you had the faintest trace of makeup, other than face powder. It was the "natural" look then without the help of cosmetics.

Girls wore scarves around their necks, not on their heads. Hats were large and made of velvet or felt. No stretch pants, on or off campus. Undergarments consisted of a corset or girdle, "Teddy Bears", (a sort of cotton chemise), and a slip, also cotton. The girls wore blouses and skirts or suits to school. The sporty blouses were middy style, worn with a large, square silk scarf, folded in a triangle and tied in front under a large collar.

A Lawrence boy would have bought his clothes at several men's stores; Ober's; Johnson & Carl; Peckham's; Robt. E. House; Winey & Underwood; Abe Wolfson; or Protch the Tailor. The suits always had a vest. The trousers were fairly narrow and the cuff came just to the top of the high top shoe—sort of high water effect. Black or brown socks matched the shoes. Boys carried pocket watches. Collars were not attached to the shirts. Stiff, white collars were fastened in the front and back of the shirt with a collar button. When the collar became soiled, it was sent to the laundry to be starched and laundered. Extra collars were kept in a round, leather collar box.

Men wore caps on the campus mostly, although a few dressier ones wore hats. A bareheaded man or woman in cold weather was unheard of. Freshmen men had to wear freshmen caps, small beanies.

The freshmen this year will arrive in cars, or fly in to Kansas City, or come by bus. Fifty years ago, they came by train. The baggage rooms at the Santa Fe and Union Pacific stations would be jammed with trunks and suit cases. Trains carried extra coaches for students going all over the country to school.

Cabs would be lined up at the stations, waiting to take the students to their rooming houses or fraternities. The cab drivers standing alongside the cab and hawking for fares, would rush up to a co-ed and grab a suit case. Trunks were sent up later in cabs, trucks or Ad Manter's transfer wagon. Today, many recognize a student arriving in town by the line of clothes hanging across the back seat of the car with either the student or a parent driving. They are on their way with those countless sweaters, skirts, dresses, slacks or shirts, to one of the many well-equipped dormitories or organized houses.

September, 1916, registration and enrollment took place in Robinson Gymnasium. Enrollees walked up the hill, or rode the street car. Walking was fashionable then. When you enrolled, if you were a sorority pledge, your sorority sisters were on hand to help you and to steer you away from any instructor who was known to be not too friendly toward social organizations.

Students had the choice of several book stores to buy books and supplies and their "memory" book, (scrap book)—Rowland's College Book Store on 14th where the Wagon Wheel cafe now is located; the University Book Store downtown; Keelers; Bell's Music Store and Pierce's Music Store for music supplies; F. I. Carter (same location as now); Morrison & Bliesner for typewriters. There was a choice of several banks—Peoples State Bank, Merchants National Bank (now called First National Bank); Watkins National Bank; Citizens State Bank; and the Lawrence National Bank. You patronized Con Squires or Alfred Lawrence to have your picture taken.

If you were a non-fraternity student, you roomed at a rooming house as close to the campus as you could. And you ate your meals at a boarding club; at Lee's College Inn, (below Rowland's); or Brick's on Oread where the Gas Light Tavern is now; or down town at the Evereat or the DeLuxe, near the Eldridge.

Even the buildings on the campus looked different in 1916. The Administration building (Strong Hall), had only one wing. Old Blake Hall with the clock is now gone, as is old Fraser. Green Hall didn't have the bronze statue in front, Spooner Library now is the Art Gallery.

"Aunt Carrie" Watson ruled the library. A large, erect woman, she used to walk regally down the rubber strip in the center aisle and admonish anyone foolish enough to be caught whispering or giggling. In fact, she was known to have sent many a culprit out of the library for such an offense.

Library dates at night were popular. Week-night dates were not permitted, but a boy could take a girl home from the library. You walked. And you were given thirty minutes to get in after library closing hours. Your date had to wait outside the library for you to come out. There always were plenty of boys to keep each other company while waiting. Of course, you always got through studying long before closing hour. And the walk home could be quite circuitous.

There will be no candy or ice cream store like Wiedemann's for this year's freshmen to frequent. Wilson's Drug Store (now Rankin's), was also a popular downtown gathering place for sodas.

No doubt there are just as handsome and "different" professors today, but it will be hard to convince the 50-year-ago freshman that there are. Take for example, D. L. Patterson; John N. Van Der Vries, and C. A. Dykstra. Most of the girls sat in the front row for their classes.

You could see W. W. Davis walking jauntily on the campus swinging his cane, or he and Professor Patterson playing golf every afternoon at the Country Club. Professor Davis' favorite expression in class was, "perfectly asinine". The student today won't have the fun of taking a quiz under Professor Blackmar and filling the quiz book to the last page by elaborating, and writing and writing—just so the book was filled and you wrote a good last paragraph.

You could call everyone in every class by name. The classes are so big and impersonal now, that students will not have the fun of walking down to Louisiana Street to Prof. Skilton's home for a 10:30 class in Music Appreciation and listening to records played.

And do students today ever answer roll call for a friend? And take turns going to class? And what professor today would dance in Greek Drama class to demonstrate Greek dancing? Professor Wilcox, with his black skull cap on his head, would do that.

Then there was Professor Cady who demonstrated making dry ice in Bailey and would end the lecture by throwing handfulls of frozen cranberries out into the audience. And is there an English professor today who can write with as precise a hand as Professor O'Leary did on your papers in "Short Story"? Professor Dunlap would read passages of Shelly & Keats and for fear you might not appreciate a special passage, would read it, look out over the class, and remark: "Now, isn't that just beautiful?" That year, 1916, saw Mrs. Eustace Brown hired as "Adviser to Women", and of course, the students promptly nicknamed her, "Mrs. Useless Brown".

The second century K. U. co-ed of today will swing down Jayhawk Boulevard, in that short, short, skirt, not impeded by the long, dark, bulky, skirts of fifty years ago. Her long, straight hair may have a tiny scarf over it, and she will have plenty of makeup on that skin that doesn't really need it. And the boy walking beside her, will have on tight, tight, stretch pants or faded jeans, a colored shirt, white socks and sloppy loafers. And he will be bareheaded.

What will student dress be 50 years from now? It is difficult to imagine.

Printed in Journal-World Sept. 16, 1966

Swimming

LAWRENCE NOW HAS A NEW, deluxe, outdoor swimming pool where the old and young, black and white, can learn to swim. The youth of yesterday had a wide choice for outdoor swimming. And those spots too, were open to all ages and color.

There was Peterson's Pond on the Lake View road. One of its "alumns" described it as the place where you got scum on your chest. The Lake View Club, six miles northwest of Lawrence, offered such attractions as water snakes in its muddy waters. You might be floating or swimming along and a fish or two would nibble at your toes. When you jumped in off the dock, your feet would touch bottom and that in itself was a sensation. Your toes would sink in soft, squashy mud. There was no beach— only the boat dock to climb up on to rest. And there were always splinters that seemed to go into places where someone else had to extract them for you.

Then there was the old Brick Yard pond at the foot of Mississippi street where the Veterans of Foreign Wars club is now. It was used for skating in winter, too. The Wakarusa river had several choice swimming spots; one was at Brown's Grove, south of Lawrence. The grove had many walnut trees, red bud, paw paw and persimmon. The banks were steep and muddy most of the time.

Deichmann's Crossing, now called "Gage Bridge", on the Wakarusa was a wonderful spot, not only for swimmers, but for picnickers. Large stone slabs on its banks eliminated the fear of poison ivy, snakes and chiggers. There was a suspension bridge over the Wakarusa somewhere between Lawrence and Eudora. It too, was a spot for swimmers.

Many a boy learned to swim in the Kaw River. There was one place near the Santa Fe station. But all along the Kaw's banks, the natural sand beach made it enticing to the young. Most of the swimming there was sans swim suits. One time there were complaints that the boys were swimming too close to the bridge, as the spectators were seeing too much of them. At the foot of Ohio Street, Dolly Graeber, the town's most respected boatman, had his boat dock. For several summers when the river was quite low, old and young came there to swim. Some of the best swimmers would swim across the river to the north side, and back.

Probably, most of the girls learned to swim in the Y.M.C.A. indoor pool. This building later was better known as the Wren building. It was built in the early 1900's at a reported cost of $40,000. At that time, it was believed there was a need in Lawrence for a place where young men could go to enjoy gymnasium facilities and a pool. It also offered rooms for bachelors. The entire project was supported by the merchants in Lawrence.

One day a week was given to girls and women who subscribed for gym and swimming lessons. Every Wednesday was our day. Returning to school after lunch, we brought our little cardboard suitcases containing our swim suit, gym bloomers, a white turkish towel, (no colored ones then), and a "Boudoir-cap" type swimming cap that always let in the water. We always found room in that suitcase for our after-swim snack—sandwiches or cookies (which we'd trade back and forth), and always pickles— dill or sour. We bought the pickles for a penny each at the Leader, where the Kraft Furniture store now is located; or Thudiums or McCurdy's. Those pickles were the size of the largest you see on the market today. We can still smell that dill when the clerk would take a long-handled cup and dip into the wooden barrel that held them. We all had the same kind of suitcase. They probbaly were purchased at Hoadley's or Miller's Racket store.

At 4 o'clock, when school was dismissed, we walked to the Y.M. and dressed for gym. Our costumes were black pleated bloomers, black stockings (cotton), and white middy blouses. The material in the bloomers was perhaps sateen. Our swiming outfits also consisted of bloomers. I have found no one who can recall the blouse. They probably were in one piece. The material in these bloomers was a heavy, wirey alpaca type.

While we took "gym", the women, and some of them our mothers, had their swimming lesson. The gymnasium was one floor above. After gym we had to slide down a brass pole to the pool area in the basement. The pool room was always chilly and damp and smelled musty. The cement floor was always slippery. We had to take a shower before we could enter the pool. It was not heated and one now wonders if the room was heated. It was hard to keep our teeth from chattering and our body from shaking, it was that cold.

Miss Douglas was our teacher. We all had to stay in the shallow end until she was ready to give us our individual lesson. This was preceded by a general group instruction or talk. Each child was given a certain amount of time for individual attention. When your time came, a long rope was tied under your arms and you had to jump in at the deep end. If anyone hesitated too long to suit Miss Douglas, she would push her in. You'd flounder around, relying heavily on the rope to hold you up, always wondering if Miss Douglas was strong enough to hold you up, or if she might slip and fall in while she was pulling you to "shore". Floating and the breast stroke were the two things we were taught first. It was a great day when we mastered the stroke and could swim across the length of the pool without the protecting rope.

The highlight of each swim day was the "feast" while we were dressing—the sharing and trading of our food. It was always 5:30 or 6 when we came out of the building to walk home. In the winter months, it would be pitch dark. The only light would be the feeble street light on the corners. Those living in the same neighborhood walked home together, with no thought of fear. Our suitcases were heavy with wet suits and towels and our long hair would be dripping, whatever the weather, hot or cold.

The men and boys had the building the rest of the week. They met regularly for gym classes. There were no gymnasiums in the public schools then. One "alumnus" recalls it cost $5 a year to join, which included everything. Basketball teams were organized for all ages. Some of the older boys then in high school, went to KU and were members of our outstanding teams.

There were two or three times during the winter months, for a gathering at supper time when the boys paid 10c for all the mush and milk they could consume.

After World War I, interest in the YMCA lagged and the building was taken over by the Chamber of Commerce. Later it was purchased by the Jackman interests and remodeled for WREN studios. At that time, the two large concrete birds were put up at the front entrance. Lastly, the building was converted into apartments, and an office for the Independent Laundry. About three years ago, fire destroyed its interior. Like so many other building "casualties" the site now is a bare parking lot.

Printed in Journal-World May 5, 1969

Beauty Shops

WHAT WOULD YOU THINK IF YOU were walking down the street
on a bright, sunny day and looked up and saw a mop of long
hair hanging out of a window? It was a common sight any sunny
day back in the early 1900's if you were walking past Mrs.
Kinnear's house at the corner of 8th and Ohio streets, where
the Bess Stone Activity Center now is. Everybody had long hair
in those days.

Mrs. Kinnear was a short, dark haired, plump widow. She
talked quite a bit. When you had your hair washed, it took a
long time because all the drying was done by hand-rubbing and
the sun. Your hair was first brushed vigorously, then soaped,
rubbed hard, and rinsed over a tin-lined bath tub. Rain water
from the cistern was soft and the castile soap lathered easily.

Mrs. Kinnear had been known to rub salt on the scalp to
stimulate it, but one young, black-haired girl, soon found she
was turning into a red-head, and that treatment was stopped at
her father's request.

Mrs. Kinnear would have you sit on a low stool and hang
your hair out the window after she rubbed your scalp good and

hard. As the sun streamed through the window on the south, you would turn first with your face out and then with your face in the room; until your hair was dry. As people walked by, towards town, they often could recognize some of the owners of the hair by the color.

It cost 25c for a shampoo including having the hair braided or "dressed". She would take several strands of hair, twist them and pin them on top of your head with hair pins. When you got home and removed the hair pins, you had a semblance of a wave. Some of the young high school girls called this process, "The Kinnear Kanob".

Not long after Mrs. Kinnear was in business, Miss Hilda Lofgren started her shop in her home in the 700 block on Kentucky Street. Hilda was a tall, blonde, angular woman, who always carried an umbrella when she walked to town, whether rain or shine, winter or summer. She rinsed your hair over a china wash bowl. The wash bowl was one of those kind with a matching pitcher and waste jar. All three pieces were used.

Hilda's widowed mother would help her by rubbing the hair dry and visiting with you with each vigorous rub, and each painful jerk of the comb trying to get the snarls out. Mrs. Lofgren was a large, strong, rather heavy woman. Once in a while, someone would whisper they had seen a male customer entering the house for scalp treatments, falling hair or receding brow, no doubt. These appointments were usually after working hours to avoid chance encounters with a lady customer.

You didn't go to a shop oftener than once a month. For home treatment, it depended upon the season of the year, how often you washed your own hair. One girl in the neighborhood had a luxurious head of hair. She shocked us one day by saying she washed her hair in water only twice a year. She brushed it every night 100 times by count, and often corn meal was rubbed in her scalp and then brushed out.

When drying your hair in the wintertime, you had to stand or sit over a floor radiator or sit by the open oven door in the kitchen. Devices for curling the hair were ingenious. Some recall cutting a tin can in strips, wrapping each strip in paper and rolling the hair over each strip. Rags were used. Either process, the hair was dampened first. Kid curlers came next. These were small pieces of wire covered with kid leather, and you bought them in a variety or department store.

By the time beauty parlors started up downtown, curling irons were used to make the round curl. The irons worked like a scissors in that the hair was put between the two tongs, and wound around the outside. The iron was heated over a lamp chimney or a stove burner. Later, the electric curling iron appeared. With these instruments, you could also curl your hair at home.

When the Marcel Wave came in, the single heavy bar had to be handled by an operator trained in knowing how to make a deep natural looking wave, and not a round curl. The bar was heated over a rectangular shaped gas burner about six or seven inches long and two inches wide. Incidentally, the Marcel Wave started in France when Mr. Marcel, a beauty operator, followed his mother's natural wave to get the natural effect. The Marcel Wave is practically a lost art today as beauty schools no longer offer it. It takes too long to learn it. When the wave was in vogue, K. U. students would get one for a big party, then hurry back to the shop in a day or two to get a retrace for another party, or between times before their next shampoo.

Mrs. Fay H. Brown, a past member of the board of the National Hairdressers and Cosmetologists Association and former State President of the Kansas Cosmetologists Association, came to Lawrence in 1927 and purchased one of the leading beauty shops down town. She said there were shops in Topeka as far back as 1895. Marcel waving was all the rage when Mrs. Brown came to Lawrence. It was followed by comb waving and finger waving. Hair pins were used to hold the wave in a finger wave. Pin curls followed, and bobby pins held the hair in place.

Permanents came in during the early 1920's. They were very expensive. In Kansas City there were only two or three shops with the reputation of not ruining your hair or burning it off. Not only were there those hazards, but you risked all of your hair possibly falling out months later, or getting your scalp burned in the process, due to excessive heat. If you felt you might be getting burned, you would signal the operator who with a bellows would blow on the hot spot.

About 1920, short hair was coming in. If you decided to make that momentous decision, whether to cut or not to cut, and you decided to cut, you had a permanent at the same time.

My first permanent was in Kansas City and it cost $35. It took a full day. Mrs. Brown says the first ones came from wrapping the hair in paper pasteboard tubes. When the paper became brown, your hair was "done". The operator would then take a pair of pliers and crack the pasteboard tubes. Many a permanent came out fuzzy. Brilliantine was used generously, to take out the fuzz and dryness of the hair.

The "Frederick" wave was considered one of the best. The price was one dollar a curl and some heads took as many as sixty curls. The spiral wave was followed by the Croquinole, in which the hair was wrapped around horizontally. The popular home permanent was the "Nestle". A set cost $15. There were five spiral rods to wrap your hair, and one electric heater. It would take five or six hours with long hair as you could only do five curls at a time.

Beauty prices in general have been steady with a gradual rise, except during the Depression. One cutrate shop here was known to have charged 15c for a shampoo and 25c for a set if you dried your hair at home. Hair drying in a shop was done first by hand, and then the arm dryer came into existence. It was portable and was moved around over the head with the operator rubbing the scalp to hasten the drying. The modern dryers today do not even need heat, but some heat is used merely for the comfort of the customer. Needless to say, they are much easier on the hair.

There were few legal restrictions on beauty shops in the early years. You could complete a beauty course in six weeks. Now it takes nine months. If you had been practicing the profession, you were exempt in taking the course. You could hang up a shingle with no experience. No license was necessary at first. The operators' uniforms have changed little, except color is now often used instead of white, and materials are mostly drip-dry. There used to be only two kinds of nail polish—clear and natural. Manicures were 50c; now they are $1.75 and up.

Going back to the early 1900's, any makeup was looked upon with disfavor. If you were known to use it, you were just not the right kind of a girl. So, you would rub your cheeks real hard, or pinch them. Red crepe paper, moistened, was rubbed on the cheeks too. One young girl living in a small town, bought rouge in Topeka where the druggist wouldn't know her or tell that she used it. Lip sticks were not in existence, so you bit your lips and moistened them often.

Instead of "teasing" the hair, you "ratted" it. Toilet water and perfume were in liquid form only. Deodorants were unheard of and when they finally came on the market, you consulted the family physician before you were allowed to use them. Beauty shops made their own liquid soap by shaving bars of castile soap and mixing the liquid in gallon glass jars. Brilliantine, to make your hair shine, was used as early as the 1890's. One home recipe was:

"Eau de Cologne	— 1 oz.
Glycerine	— 1 oz.
Clarified honey	— 2 oz.
Rectified spirit	— 4 oz."

and if you think curling fluid is recent, back in 1890 was this home recipe:

"1 oz. borax
1 drachm gum arabic
1 pt. hot water
2 T. camphor."

Hair coloring was sub rosa. It was done to cover up the telltale grey hairs. Rinses and bleaches and dyeing were all done behind closed curtains. Lemon juice, paroxide, and camamile tea were used for blondes, either at home or in the shop.

Wigs were rare in those early days. And if they were worn, it was a dead secret. Today, the modern woman comes into the shop carrying her smart looking wig case, discusses how she wants her wig styled, and makes the appointment when to pick it up. The price is at least double the regular price for a shampoo and set. The re-do is done on an average of once a month. Wigs are a convenience today for the woman who wants to swim in the daytime and dance that night.

One K. U. alumnus visiting in California this summer, met a former sorority sister of some forty years back. The first night they were at a party together, she was a blonde; the next time they met, she was chestnut haired; and the third time, a redhead. The lady was never caught in swimming, so the visitor is still wondering whether her real hair is grey or white. "Only her hairdresser would know for sure."

Printed in Journal-World Nov. 12, 1965

Lawrence in Summertime

IN THE EARLY 1900's, before air conditioners, and electric fans in the homes, Lawrence could be pretty hot in summertime. However, you adjusted to the weather, and the long summers sped by quickly for young people. Little girls' curls disappeared, the hair was parted in the middle and two tight braids took their place. Each pig tail was tied at the end with a colored ribbon bow. Your hair was pulled back so tight, your head would be sore when you unbraided it at night to brush your hair before going to bed. Sometimes a tight bun was rolled over each ear and pinned in place by hair pins. Everybody had long hair in those days.

With warmer weather you discarded your black stockings, socks were not known then, and went barefoot all day. Some of us had to wear sandals or moccasins to protect our feet from glass or nails. Blue jeans were worn universally by both girls and boys. But they were called, "overalls" and they had a bib attached with adjustable buckles on the straps or suspenders. The bib was high enough so that you did not have to wear a blouse or shirt underneath. This type of apparel was for the "pre-teens" only.

Along about ten o'clock each morning, doors and windows of the houses were closed, and the shutters or the dark green blinds drawn, to keep the house as cool as possible. Women and girls took afternoon naps and on real hot days, a pallet was made on the living room floor. It was cooler than upstairs. Everybody stayed indoors until along about four or five o'clock. Then baths in the tin-lined tub were taken and you would dress for supper and the evening's activities.

There were no summer playgrounds or Scout camps in those days. You devised your own entertainment. Sometimes it would only be sitting on the curbing in front of your house and having a friendly contest with your friends across the street, in mud ball throwing. This always took place after a good rain the night before—dirt streets, you know. Saplings were cut or torn off of a young tree sprout or shrub and mud balls were rolled and stuck on the end. The idea was to see how far you could toss the mud ball. Distance, and not the friend, was the target.

In the evenings, parades on the sidewalks, with lighted shoe boxes, were held by all the children in the neighborhood. You spent days fixing up these boxes. Cutouts of all shapes were made on the sides of the boxes, and then the open "windows" were pasted over with colored tissue paper. You had four or five boxes in your "train", and some were made with two stories. All were joined by heavy string and pulled. In each box was placed a candle and after dark, the candles were lighted and the parade began. This took up several weeks of a summer.

There always were paper dolls and Jacks for the girls to fall back on. The paper dolls were cutouts from fashion magazines. One magazine was used to file the dolls, separated as to members of the family, and then their various wardrobes. If you played Jacks, with a golf ball instead of the usual hard rubber ball, you really "rated".

Marbles and "mumbledy peg" were the popular games for the boys. When they played these, they had to wear leather knee caps tied around the legs over the long black stockings, so that no holes were worn in the stockings. "Mumbledy peg" was a game of dexterity. With the blade of your pocket knife exposed, you tossed the knife from various positions, for the blade to light and stick straight up in the ground or on the wooden sidewalk.

The Kaw river had its attractions in summer as well as winter. Boys swam there, or in the Brick Yard pond, and later in Potter Lake. If you were lucky and knew someone whose father belonged to the Lake View Club, a club six miles north and west of Lawrence, you swam there. Fishing and boating took place there too. Boating was popular with the K. U. students in spring and summer. Fraternities would take their dates up the river in several boat loads. They would stop at a sand bar, tie the boats together, and drift down the river, singing fraternity and popular songs. Needless to say, these parties were normally organized on moonlight nights.

There were Regattas too, for all ages. They started at the foot of Ohio street. One summer there were 1,000 spectators. The events included a canoe race between the KU team and the Blue River Canoe Club of Kansas City. KU won "by a nose", on a quarter mile course in two minutes and fifteen seconds. Other events at that Regatta:

> Single canoe.
> 100-yard swim. Winner—Clarence Stevens, first;
> > Joe Bishop, second; Ben Carman, third.
> Canoe mixed double.
> Row boat mixed double.
> Speed launches—Weyermiller's Daffodil, first.
> Long Dive—Sam Maffett.
> Tilting Match.
> Tub race, won by Frank Benedict.
> Motor speed race, won by George Savage's Momus over
> > the Van Hoesen boat.

Fourth of July was always a big day for all ages. The fire crackers seemed louder then. "Cannon crackers" were the loudest and biggest. People would walk up and down Massachusetts Street shooting off crackers, but the deadliest and most terrifying, were the canes. A cap was inserted in the bottom of a special kind of cane, and as you walked along, boys and men would walk up in back of you and tap the cane on the cement walk at your ankles and the explosion and noise would result.

July 4, 1900, there was an all-day Community picnic at Miller's Grove. We presume Miller's Grove was where the Miller house is on east 19th, where the Leo Ellers now live. Buch's Band and the Arcade Glee Club performed. The band gave a concert before and after the fireworks at Woodward's Corner, which is the present site of the Round Corner Drug Store. The fireworks were shot off at the Eldridge House corner too.

In June, 1901, Massachusetts Street was brick paved for the first time. Parades from then on could be held without worry of rains and mud. The "Floto Shows" gave a street parade in 1903 and the performances were on "South Kentucky Street." "Ben Hur's Herd of Arabian Stallions, 100 Shetland Ponies," acrobats, monkeys, Salambo and Scotch Collie dogs, and clowns, were offered for entertainment. Young people would get up before dawn and walk to the railroad station to watch the circus unload, then follow it to the circus grounds and watch the men pitch the tents.

There were matinee horse races for adults, all summer at the Driving Park track. This track was a little north of the Mall off of 23rd Street.

In the early 1900's, the Airdome was a popular night attraction. High school girls went in groups or line parties, as did the boys. No dates for these. Admission was 10c. Stock companies played to capacity crowds despite the odor wafting from Moak's Livery stable next door to the north. The "theatre" was a large tent with canvas top and sides. The sides were rolled up but could be quickly dropped if a storm blew in. Seats were long, hard, wooden benches. The tent was in a vacant lot in the 700 block of Vermont, on the east side where the Telephone Company office building is now. The plays changed their repertoire once a week.

One ad in the Lawrence Journal of 1909, gave this notice: "The Martin Stock Company will present, "The Mill Owner's Daughter", a comedy drama in four acts. In the last act of this bill, takes place one of the greatest sensational fights ever produced on the American stage. Don't miss it. Try to get in." All of the June bugs, and moths, and mosquitoes around the lights, couldn't have kept you away.

One summer, instead of a stock company, a Merry-Go-Round was set up on the lot. In the process of assembling it, a worker broke his arm. He was rushed across the street to Dr. A. J. Anderson's office. After the arm was set, the man asked "A. J." how much he owed him. The reply was: "You can pay me by letting my three kids ride free on your Merry-Go-Round all summer". And they did just that!

If you couldn't think of anything else to do and it was a hot, sultry night, you took the street car and paid your five-cent fare, and rode around the "Loop". The summer street cars were open on both sides and you could count on a good breezy ride.

Ice Cream socials had their place in the summertime too. They were usually sponsored by a Ladies Aid Society. Tables and chairs were set out on the lawn. Japanese lanterns were strung around the yard and were lighted, first by candles, and later by electricity. Home made ice cream, or Wiedemann's, or Zuttermeister's, was served, and home made cake. Sometimes these ice cream socials were on the night of a band concert and close to one of the parks. Most often, they were on a Saturday night, when the stores were open for business, and shoppers were out.

Ice Cream wagons roamed the streets in summer. Jerry Ewers had a horse-drawn wagon and at the band concerts and other places where a crowd might be, he would sell ice cream, peanuts and pop corn. He made some sort of waffle-like cone while you waited, that he rolled while still hot, and he would fill it with ice cream. All of this for five cents.

Some summers would develop into quite a social season for the high school and college age girls. Quite often nieces and friends would come for a visit. There would be thimble parties, picnics, slumber parties and line parties to the "Nickel" movie theatre, or "Patee's". The girls would bring their needlework to the thimble parties. Embroidering, crocheting lace, hemstitching, and monogramming, were popular. This work would be put on tea napkins, towels, pillow cases and lunch cloths. No knitting was learned until World War I.

Then all too soon, it would be time to go back to school.

Printed in Journal-World June 23, 1965.

Liquor in the Prohibition Era

SESSIONS OF THE KANSAS LEGISLATURE these days usually take up the subject of liquor by the drink. This is a far cry from the days of national prohibition. It brings to mind the many devious ways people used to get around the law then. Bootleggers abounded. But it wasn't too easy to buy liquor in those days. You had to know the right people or have friends who passed you the word where to get it. And in turn, in Lawrence the bootlegger had to know about your integrity in not advertising his existence.

Lawrence had numerous methods of delivering liquor. A cornfield was one contact. Then there was "Aunt Jane" who lived in east Lawrence and supplied many a student. Pittsburg had its "deep shaft" whiskey. In fact, that whiskey was delivered as far east as New York City. A Lawrence man made that discovery when he was there and was being entertained.

Nearby Leavenworth used a milk wagon for delivery. The liquor was bottled in milk bottles that were painted white inside, so the contents looked like milk. The story goes that the expression, "Bathtub Gin" got its origin from Leavenworth. They claimed that many a gallon of gin was mixed in bath tubs in officers quarters.

One of our friends traveled for a living and Wichita was on his route. While down there one week, he was warned by his friends to be careful of bootleg whiskey made around there, because some people had been blinded by drinking it. It had too much fusel oil in it. When he returned home that weekend, he and his wife attended a dinner party where whiskey was served in cocktails. The man cautioned all of the guests about the danger of fusel oil. After the party, the family retired for the night. Several hours later, the husband awoke. He pulled the light cord by his bed to get up. All was darkness to him. He panicked. He woke his wife and said, "Honey, I'm blind. I must have gotten too much fusel oil. I turned on the light and I can't see a thing. Call the doctor. I'm blind!" She sleepily said, "Oh, that. The bulb burned out last night and I forgot to put in a new one. Go back to sleep."

Then it became the thing to do, to make your own wine and beer and gin. Whiskey was never attempted. The beer making was taken on as a community enterprise among close friends. Huge pottery jars, bottling caps and bottles were purchased. Drug stores advertised the various ingredients to make the beer, and the tools to make and bottle it. There were many discussions by the men as to which brand of malt was the best and where you could buy it the cheapest. The men figured how much a bottle the stuff cost. All brands of malt were tried. Each man had his favorite kind.

The beer had to work so long, and then when it reached a certain temperature, it had to be bottled immediately. If you were to be away for the evening, there would be a quick last minute trip to the cellar to figure how many hours you could be gone. Sometimes the man would leave a party and take one or two friends with him to help bottle, and then they would come back to the party. The women had nothing to do with any of the operations. It was strictly a male project.

One time a bottle of beer was opened in our kitchen. It must have gotten too warm. The stuff shot out like "Old Faithful", and we had to have our kitchen repainted. Sometimes the beer would explode in the basement where the bottles were shelved. You might be sitting upstairs quietly playing Bridge when a loud popping would be heard from the cellar area. If the man of the house was home, one wild dash to the cellar would take place. One time, one of the men took an umbrella with him to protect himself from flying glass. Beer making did have its hazards.

Wine making followed. Dandelion, wheat, wild elderberry and wild grape, all were tried. Everybody exchanged recipes and samples. But domestic grape was the most successful and popular. Again, wine presses were bought, clean barrels purchased from the Poehler Mercantile Company, and syrup barrels from the drug stores. Quite a few grapes were grown in those years in and around Lawrence.

A few times, several merchants got together and bought a carload of grapes to be shipped from California. Then there was much activity as the grapes had to be used before they spoiled.

One thing was for sure, you always knew who was making wine, because the minute you stepped in a house, those little gnats that fly around fruit, would greet you at the front door.

Then there were the gin makers. The alcohol was obtained from bootleggers or bootleg drug stores. Once in a while, a doctor friend would write a prescription for pure grain alcohol and you got it filled at a certain drug store in Kansas City. It was legal to sell juniper oil. The gin was supposed to be better the more you mixed the alcohol, juniper oil and distilled water. It was common practice for many to have a half gallon bottle under the back seat of your car. The jolting and vibrations of the car did the mixing for you.

It may be hard to believe, but it would appear that these consumers of 40 years ago, have survived with no ulcers, at least not many, that is.

Printed in Journal-World Jan. 10, 1968

Lawrence History

THE EARLY HISTORY OF LAWRENCE and Kansas was filled with a struggle for the defense of high principles. At first, the New Englanders came, determined to make it a free state, unrestricted by race or color, and were followed a few years later by many Germans from the Old Country who came to escape military service and to start a new life of freedom. The early days were filled with border wars, guerilla raids, grasshopper scourges, and in later years, floods.

In the early part of 1854, the feeling of anti-slavery was running high throughout the north, and when the Kansas-Nebraska bill was passed in May 25, 1854, providing that the people themselves should decide whether Kansas should be slave or free, those Free-Staters were determined that slavery was not going to secure a foothold in new territory. It was feared because of its proximity to Missouri, which was a strong pro-slave state, that Kansas territory would turn to slavery. The New England Emigrant Aid Society was formed in Massachusetts to encourage and aid emigration to Kansas, and Amos L. Lawrence of Boston was one of its prominent leaders. In June, 1854, they sent Dr. Charles Robinson of Fitch (he was later to become Kansas' first governor), and Mr. Charles H. Branscomb of Holyoke, to pick out a site for the colony. Dr. Robinson had stood on Mount Oread (where the University now stands), when he went to California in the gold rush of '49, and remembered its beautiful view, so he picked it for a townsite.

The first contingent arrived by train at St. Louis August 1, 1854 and Dr. Robinson met them. They took a steamer up the Missouri River to Kansas City, and then the final 40 miles to Lawrence on foot. Ox teams were used to carry their baggage.

The group left Kansas City at 10 o'clock on Saturday evening and arrived in Lawrence on Tuesday. It was hot going, so most of the traveling was done at night. Now it takes less than 45 minutes to cover the same distance.

Twenty-five tents were pitched on Mount Oread the night of arrival and the colonizers all voted in favor of the site. However, a few days later they moved down and camped near the Kaw or Kansas river, where the town continued to grow south of the river. In September, a larger group came, and from then on small bands of settlers continued to filter in and settle down in Lawrence.

Lawrence did not start out being called "Lawrence". The settlers tried several names, such as Waukarusa (the Waukarusa river is south of the town), Yankeetown, Excelsior, New Boston, and finally Lawrence in honor of Amos A. Lawrence of Boston.

The people of Missouri were determined Kansas was going to be a slave state, and Lawrence being the headquarters of the Free-State party and the center of the free movement, naturally became the focal point of conflict and bloodshed and destruction waged time after time between the border ruffians and the free-staters. When the first election was held for the territorial legislature, hundreds of Missourians came over and registered and voted so that the entire legislature, with one exception, had been elected by Missourians. All subsequent elections were conducted the same way and voters were influenced by threat of death and destruction. Feeling ran high and bitter. Appeals were made to the territorial governors, to Congress, and to the eastern sponsors, but due to distance, politics, and misrepresentation, nothing much could be done to help the free-staters, and the pro-slaveryites gained control of the militia.

The sheriff, S. J. Jones, was a Missouri ruffian who had been appointed by the Kansas territorial governer to keep law and order in Lawrence. Thus the free-staters had to exert great caution not to overstep the law and provide an excuse to kill some of their leaders. One man was sent to Boston to lay the matter before the friends of free Kansas, and as a result, rifles were smuggled into Lawrence, in anticipation of bloodshed that was bound to come.

In May of 1856, the town was looted and the Free-State Hotel (present site of the Hotel Eldridge) was burned to the ground. Conflict and bloodshed in retaliation followed, first by the free-staters led by John Brown, and then by the pro-slavers. These constant conflicts bound the people of Lawrence closer together.

Before the town was given a charter, all necessary business to carry on the mechanics of a town was done voluntarily by each man carrying out his duties and working with the others without meetings, and by word agreement only, as they had no legal authority until a charter would be granted. Troops were sent out by Governor Walker in 1857 to dispel any power that might be displayed, or any signs that might show organization, but the troops could find none. It was all done so unobstrusively and quietly by suggestion only, that they could find nothing that indicated the setting up of an independent city government.

Finally, after numerable bogus elections, the free-state people gained control of the territorial legislature and one of the first things considered was a charter for Lawrence. A bill was passed February 11, 1858 and on February 20, the charter was accepted and city officers were elected.

Women played an important role in the early days. They took a hand in everything and did their share of the work. They came to Kansas with the full understanding of what they had to meet. They helped provide rations and make bullets. They were womanly and had been reared in cultured homes, but they had strong convictions and devoted their lives to maintaining them.

In the years 1857 and 1858, the State had appeared so much in the papers that it was popular to come to Kansas. Emigrants from all over moved to Kansas to help. Many college students turned from a literary life to come to Lawrence, not for personal gain, but for a principal, to help make it free. Not only emigrants came, but many others to see the country. They nearly all had money and they had it to spend.

There was not much productivity in Lawrence at that time, but a good deal of building was in progress and Lawrence enjoyed a wave of business prosperity. Colonel S. W. Eldridge and his brother built a 4-story brick hotel at a cost of $80,000 on the site of the Free-State hotel that had been burned to the ground by raiders. Many churches were built. Then from September 1859 to October 1860 a drouth swept over the state. Lawrence suffered less than some of the newer sections, due partly to aid received from Illinois and other prosperous states.

January 29, 1861 Kansas became a state and the legislature passed a bill submitting the question of the permanent capitol to the vote of the people. Lawrence and Topeka were the two competitors, and in the ensuing election, Lawrence lost.

New troubles started shortly. Civil War was declared and Lawrence was in a hot spot. Being only 40 miles from the Missouri border, she was in the center of "Border ruffian" hate. Lawrence people realized they were vulnerable to raids and that it still rankled the ruffians that they had been repulsed in the years back, and they were afraid they would some day be attacked in reprisal. Then too, Lawrence had the reputation in Missouri and in pro-slave states of being one of the stations of the underground railroad. Many slaves made their way to Lawrence and were given help, although it was not admitted at the time.

The negroes made good citizens of the community and they were healthy and eager to work and were self-sustaining. Since they were eager to learn, a night school was started for them; the teaching was done on a volunteer basis and without recompense. It was conducted in the form of a Sabbath school.

Meanwhile, guerilla bands roamed all over Missouri. The most famous leader was Quantrill. William Clark Quantrill was born in Ohio of good parents. His father was a school teacher. Quantrill came to Kansas at the age of 20. He taught school near Stanton for a year, then went to Salt Lake for two years and in 1860 he returned and made headquarters at Lawrence. When he came to Lawrence he went by the name of Charlie Hart. He carried on questionable dealings and came to the attention of the Law. He fled to Missouri and proceeded to carry on numerous raids and killings and soon became the most dangerous of the guerilla leaders.

By 1863 Quantrill had become very bold, and sacked communities and farms as he pleased. Efforts were made to protect Lawrence. A military company was organized, arms were secured from the State, but the colonel in charge had a peculiar notion that all arms should be kept in the armory and not at home.

Lawrence felt reasonably safe, regardless of repeated warnings that Quantrill would some day come there, because they thought they would be warned long before he could reach the 40-mile distance from the border. But at daybreak on August 21, 1863 Quantrill, with around 400 men, rode into Lawrence. It was one of the most brutal raids in history. He was said to have told his men that not a man in Lawrence was to be alive when they got off of their horses.

The band split up and took separate sections of the town, so that every section got its full share of murder and theft and fire. For 4 hours they ransacked and burned and murdered. As the firearms were all locked in the armory, there was no chance for the citizens to organize and defend the town. The raiders shot down every man and boy in sight and those that did not offer resistance fared as badly as others. Not one of their own men was killed.

The Eldridge hotel seemed to be regarded as the citadel of the town and the raiders descended on it in one body. They fired upon it and burned it to the ground. Buildings and homes all over the country-side were also destroyed. When the raiders rode out of town, they left a trail of fire and over 150 dead men, and many wounded. Lawrence was stunned. Only one building on Massachusetts street, the main business street, was left standing. Not even enough food was left for a day's use so thoroughly was the destruction. In the evening, as word got around, farmers who has escaped the path of the raiders, brought food and supplies for the sufferers.

In the days that followed, money poured in from cities which had heard of the devastation and money was offered and loaned without interest to those wanting to rebuild. After burying their dead and cleaning up the debris, the residents seemed more determined than ever to stay, and they set out to build better and larger buildings. In a few weeks, two companies of United States troops were sent and they remained to guard Lawrence until the end of the war. The State seal reads, "Ad Astra per Aspera" — (To the Stars through Difficulties.)

97 Years of Rushing at KU

FOR 97 YEARS, FRATERNITY AND SORORITY rushing has taken place at K.U. But the changes have been many. There were four women's fraternities by 1902. (We were taught to call them "Womens Fraternities".) Pi Beta Phi — Kappa Alpha Theta — Kappa Kappa Gamma—and Chi Omega were there in 1902, and it was ten years later before another "national" came on the campus.

Rushing started out those 97 years ago, by some of the members approaching the father of the rushee to see if he would consent to his daughter joining. If he disapproved, the girl was not asked. A sorority was purely a social organization in those years. Thirty years later, emphasis was placed more on grades and campus activities. When the Pan Hellenic Council was formed, set rules were established for rushing.

In the summertime, selected high school seniors were entertained. In Lawrence they were invited to picnics, hikes to Cameron's Bluff, Lake View, or line parties to the Airdome. Actives living over the state, wrote letters all summer to rushees coming up to school. Official rushing began in the fall and the first date would be made for a "Train Date". Transportation to Lawrence was entirely by train and the rushee would be met at the train by several "sisters". Her trunks would be loaded on the horse-drawn express truck and she would get into a hack, also horse-drawn, to be taken to her temporary home until she pledged some sorority. The day of pledging she would move her things to her chosen sorority house.

Staying at the right house was important from the sorority standpoint. The hosts could exert a lot of influence by putting their favorite sorority in a good light. Alumnae played a powerful part in rushing, not only in helping rush, but in dictating who should be rushed. Lawrence girls as members were an extra dividend. No town girls lived in a sorority house, but their fathers helped on money problems and gave the sorority good credit rating in town.

The University had no voice in sorority rushing rules. All rules were made by Pan Hellenic which consisted of two representatives from each chapter. Dances, teas, and dinners took up many days of fun and excitement. The rushing rules were strict, but it did not prevent many a rushee from being "spiked" (pledged sub rosa) before official bid day. She was given the sorority colors to pin to her garter or maybe on her camisole. In those days, sisters always pledged what the older sister had joined. And she was usually "spiked" so she could try to influence some hard-to-get rushee.

The same tradition prevailed in the fraternities. If a boy did not want to go to the same fraternity as his brothers, family pressure was brought to bear and he would know he would cause a lot of unhappiness if he did not go the family way.

A "preferential dinner" took place the night before the bids went out. The girls attending were practically "sewed up" for that sorority, but some of the most sought after girls, would perhaps go to another house after the dinner. Formal bids to join were addressed and delivered in person to the rushee. A representative of each sorority rode in the "Bid Wagon" to deliver the written bid to the candidate. The "Bid Wagon" was a tally ho drawn by four spirited horses — two white leading two black. It seated eight people and it was hired from Donnelly's Livery stable. It was quite a thrill for a rushee nervously waiting, to hear the clatter of horses hoofs on the brick pavement and see the tally ho drawing up with a flourish to deliver her bid.

When automobiles became more prevalent, bids were taken around by each sorority in a member's car. Still later, when preferential bidding came into effect, the rushee went to Strong Hall where a table was set up in the hall, manned by rush captains or alumnae, and her bid was handed out to her.

The University of Kansas and a sorority had a special appeal to many parents. They took the place of a finishing school for their daughter. Often the latter was beyond the reach of their pocketbooks.

There were no dormitories then and a rooming house for their shielded offspring did not seem to carry the social prestige nor protection of a sorority and its housemother. A housemother in those days functioned as genteel hostess, housekeeper and watch-dog over the girls. Thirty to thirty-five members were capacity for a house, as against 70 and up today. During the World War I years, fraternities and sororities had a hard time, financially and membership-wise. The boys were at war and the girls didn't come to college.

A contract with a house mother read like this: "It is necessary to provide a Matron whose duties shall be: First: To act as chaperone. Second: To be responsible for the cooking and serving and ordering of the meals at the time specified by an authorized member of the Fraternity. Third: To be responsible for the cleaning of all rooms on the first floor, bath rooms, hallways and such general cleaning and renovating as may be necessary. Therefore, in consideration of the party of the first part agreeing to pay the party of the second part the sum of Twenty Dollars per month with board and furnished room, from September 10, 1909 to June 10, 1910 inclusive —".

Nothing like this today. Now there is some kind of informal letter of agreement, and the salary is somewhere around $250 to

$300 a month. The house mother still chaperones parties and most of them still plan the meals and supervise the help.

Closing hours rules used to be 10 p.m. on week nights. The house would then be locked up (by the house mother), and the only way a girl could get in later than that, would be by the fire escape or wake up her roommate to let her in. Today, there is a "Security Hour" of 10:30 p.m. when the front door is locked. Every girl has a key and she sets her own hours.

Serenades from menfolk were popular after closing hours in the old days, even just a few years back. Now, that romantic tradition is no longer. They might not find anybody but the house mother at home.

Rushing is now under the guidance of the Dean of Women's office of the University. Her office works with the Pan Hellenic Council. Every rushee pays a $5 fee to register for rushing. She must be a Sophomore or upper classman to be eligible and she has to call at each of the 13 sorority houses the first day of rushing. The hours are from 9 to 4. This year all of the rushees will stay at the Holiday Inn together.

Printed in Journal-World August 21, 1970

Christmas

SOMEONE SAID "MEMORIES ARE A PART OF CHRISTMAS". As you look back on your youth at Christmas time, what do you remember as outstanding? Your stocking caps you used to wear? Long underwear? Long black stockings? Mrs. Charlie Esterley's single seated sleigh drawn by her beautiful bay? And if you were "hooking" rides behind a delivery wagon, she would stop and have you leave your sled on the parking and you and your companion would sit beside her, tucked in with a fur robe, and away you'd go with the sleigh bells merrily ringing. She might have admonished you gently that it was pretty dangerous to be riding in back of the milk trucks and wagons. Or do you remember the new skates you got and were looking forward to skating on the river every night after school? Or how good it felt to be standing on the register in the hall when you'd come in from making "snow angels" or playing fox and geese and your feet, numb from the cold, would start to tingle as warmth began to finally flow through them.

Perhaps you remember the Christmas Eve play at the church, or when Santa came to your house on Christmas Eve and you had to wait until the stores down town had closed (around 10 o'clock sometimes) so Father, Grandfather and Uncle could be home when the parlor door was opened to reveal the Christmas tree that revolved by the heat of dozens of candles. And you had pressed your face against the front window of the dining room and watched the lamp lighter on the corner with his long handled lighter, light the light on the parking across the street and the flames would give out its feeble, eery light. (Those same lights can again be seen in the front drive of many a home in Lawrence today, but they burn perpetually now). When the men would finally arrive, there was much excitement. First there would be a knocking on a window and a deep, gruff, strange voice would ask if all the children had been good. You knew this was Santa's helper and that only good children received gifts. You were too excited and a tiny bit frightened to answer and your mother would vouch for you. Someone would then ring the small school bell that was only rung on this special occasion. The parlor door that had been kept closed and had been forbidden territory for several days before, now was wide open and the beautiful tree was ablaze and turning merrily around. All the children would march in single file and everybody would join hands and circle the tree, singing "Oh Tannenbaum".

Do you remember your first really big doll? Maybe she was of beautiful bisque, with real blond hair and big blue eyes that opened and shut. Or the tiny red enamel Swiss watch to be worn hanging on a Fluer-de-lis pin and the card for the first time said, "From Grandma and Grandpa" instead of "From Santa". Or when you were old enough to partake of the wine and Christmas cookies that always followed the opening of the packages. Christmas day was spent going around the neighborhood looking at gifts of your friends, tasting the different kinds of Christmas cookies and home made candies tied to the trees. A scissors was kept handy on the mantle for that purpose.

Do you remember?

Printed in Journal-World December 5, 1959

Wiedemann's

HOT SUMMER AFTERNOONS and nights, bring to mind the days of the ice cream parlors. The two most popular in Lawrence were Zuttermeisters and Wiedemann's. Zuttermeisters was located in the 700 block on Mass. St. on the west side. Wiedemann's was in the 800 block.

When one mentions Wiedemann's, it brings up a variety of memories. To some, the vanilla ice cream that was so rich and good, it stuck to the roof of your mouth—to others, the candy—oyster stews—Rotary and Kiwanis weekly lunches—Music Club meetings—Tea dances—and beer and cokes. Perhaps you thought Wiedemann's started and ended at the same spot—835 Massachusetts—as the stone marker on the face of the building reads, "1886". But it didn't start there.

Sometime before 1868, there was a confectionery store at 11 East 8th street. Two gentlemen under the firm name of Harris and Terry, were the owners. In 1868, William Wiedemann, father of the Wm. Wiedemann we know, bought out Mr. Terry who had previously bought out his partner, Harris. Two years after that, Mr. Wiedemann moved to 833 Massachusetts street. At that time, he sold toys and confectionary. In 1879, the elder Wiedemann died and his son, William, took over the business. In 1886 the store was moved to 835 Mass. and there business went along under the name of Wiedemann's until the early 1940's.

When the store was last moved to 835 Mass., it is presumed the soda fountain was installed and the toy business abolished. In those early years, the ice cream was made outside the back of the store. It was frozen literally by horse power. A horse was hitched to the freezer and as he walked around and around, the ice cream was frozen.

In those early years, candy and ice cream stood out more than the social life that revolved around the store. When you were given a box of Wiedemann's chocolates, it was a special something. The boxes were covered with white, shiny paper, and across the top in gold lettering "Wm. Wiedemann". The contents of the box were arranged colorfully. Square pieces the size of a caramel, chocolate creams, some pieces covered with silver or gold foil, violet colored crystal-like mints that tasted like violet, green leaf-shaped mints that were mint flavored. And all through the box were scattered those tiny French, many-colored, many-flavored candies filled with perfume.

The two most popular chocolates were the chocolate squares of fudge-like substance, topped with cocoanut and the vanilla creams that were called, "Cleveland's Choice". That name came from the fact that President Grover Cleveland had one time visited Lawrence. He was presented a box of Wiedemann's chocolates and reportedly he thought the creams the best he had ever eaten. For years after that, the candy maker refused to divulge the recipe for the filling. In fact, even the subsequent owners of Wiedemann's never knew what the filling consisted of.

Other popular candies were, the taffies that were sold only in winter. When it was cold enough to make the taffy, the taffy pulling machine which was hand operated, was brought up and placed in the south front window and taffy was pulled to show the people that the taffy season had started. Black walnut, vanilla, chocolate and molasses were placed in large metal trays and put in the show case. When you bought taffy, the clerk used a small hammer to break it into smaller pieces for easy eating.

Ribbon candy was another favorite. Once a year, Wiedemann's made small baskets of ribbon candy and filled them with fondant-covered fresh fruit. The colors of the fondant matched the fruit—orange segments and green grapes. These baskets were made on special order for the Knights Templars' New Year's Eve dinner party held in their club rooms on the fifth (top) floor of the old Lawrence National Bank building.

Wiedemann's ice cream was even richer than the present French ice cream. Maple Mousse was a favorite and fresh peach —fresh strawberry—in season—any one for 10c a dish—and it was a big dish. Ice cream sandwiches—2 for 5c—were popular. They were made at the counter on order. A layer of ice cream was placed between two thin wafers similar to a Nabisco without the filling. We'd often sit on those high stools at the fountain to make sure the fountain boy who was a friend, would give us an extra bit of ice cream, with a little persuasion. When Grape Nuts cereal came into use, Wiedemann's served "Brown Bread Ice Cream" which was made with the cereal. This was served by the slice the size of a piece of bread, and we believe it too was 5c a slice.

All sorts of shapes of lead molds were on hand for special orders of ice cream for parties and special events—hearts for Valentines—Christmas bells and Santa, flowers of all kinds, wedding bells. The appropriate color was used and you had your choice of flavor.

Hot chocolate with a big scoop of whipped cream before marshmallows were used, was a winter treat for 5c. Oyster stew in season was served with the real oyster crackers. Chili for 10c and Banana Splits for 15c came in a little bit later. Fruit salad was a special for 10c—"Sayso Cones" were 5c—egg malted milk, 15c, and phosphates 5c. These were the days before Cokes. One menu listed Tailor Made Ginger Ale under Headache Reliefs, for 5c, as also "Bromo" and "Caffiene".

The store was quite large, running back about 75 feet. As you entered, you walked on a tile floor made up of tiny round pieces of tile. On your right was the long fountain with the high stools. On the left, immediately as you entered, was Mr. Wiedemann's "office". It consisted of a desk and chair placed on a small open platform. About three feet from the floor, was a brass rod that supported dark green velvet curtains to cover up the platform. From that vantage point, Mr. Wiedemann could look over the entire store. Next to this platform was a cashier's cage where Miss Adelle Weyermuller, Mr. Wiedemann's niece presided.

After Miss Weyermuller's marriage to Otto Newby, Miss Nettie Weil (later Mrs. Clyde Teter), was cashier.

The candy counters came next, with the walnut shelves in the back holding ribbon candy and stick candy in glass jars, and candy boxes. The candy and soda fountain area were separated from the ice cream parlor by three large, carved wooden arches. Here the floor was covered by carpet and the furnishings were white marble-topped tables and ice cream chairs. In summer, big ceiling fans revolved slowly to cool the room. Black belts ran back and forth on the ceiling to rotate the paddle-like blades of these fans.

The Wiedemann family lived on the second floor and visitors climbed a long steep flight of stairs to get there. There was an outside and inside entrance. Miss Louise Wiedemann, Mr. Wiedemann's daughter, taught piano in her studio up there. She organized a pupils' music club. At the meetings, she would tell stories about the lives of composers, or tell the story part of operas. The meetings were well attended, partly because the refreshments were always ice cream—her treat.

We always looked upon Mr. Wiedemann with a little bit of awe. Anyone owning such a wonderful store commanded respect and awe, and he got it. After his death, the store was sold to Mrs. Pollock sometime in 1916.

In the winter of 1920, Richard H. Wagstaff became the owner. A new era for Wiedemann's began. Major changes were made in the physical plant and in operation. Candy and ice cream making continued, but a Tea Room and a Grill were added. Dances were inaugurated in the Grill room. Booths were installed. The second floor was converted into a Tea room. An opening was cut on the south wall of the ice cream parlor where the Grill and kitchen were added. They extended to the back of the next two buildings to the south.

The Lawrence Music Club held their meetings there, as did Rotary and Kiwanis (35c for lunch). Women entertained with luncheons and cards.

Mr. R. B. Wagstaff, father of the owner, had charge of the catering. It continued to be 'the" place to go for entertainment and good food. Tea dances were popular with the University crowd. Some of the regular frequenters were accused by some of their less frivolous friends of being "Tea Hounds". All of the popular KU bands played there at one time or another. "Swede" Wilson, Eric Owen and "Shanty" Newhouse were popular. Piano-playing "Chuck" Shofstall had "Buddy" Rogers as his drummer. Tike Kearney—Tommy Johnston—Frank Isenhart and Bob Jenks —all played there. No admittance was charged for the dances. A free-will collection was taken for the band players. Later, a 50c charge was made and all of the money went to the band.

Then followed the years of spiked beer. The students would buy "Pale Beer" which was one-half of one percent alcohol and sneak in a small bottle of alcohol without the knowledge of the proprietor. They would pour a little into the beer, then mix it by placing a thumb over the open end of the bottle and turning it upside down. During these times, the Grill was patronized mostly by KU students. But Wiedemann's never lost its air of genteelness. In those college years, if there was to be a "Night Shirt" parade, Wiedemann's would make up more ice cream than usual, sometimes to be given free to the student participants.

After prohibition was abolished, the KU beer days at Wiedemann's were over. The Grill became the popular gathering place for high school boys and girls. Dancing by Juke box and Cokes were the attraction.

Wiedemann's was probably the first commercial air-cooled establishment in Lawrence. Mr. Wagstaff conceived the idea of water cooling from a well in the creamery across the alley, which he owned also. After this was installed, women would come for sandwiches or lunch and stay all afternoon and play bridge because it was the coolest place in town. During those hot summers, the only other cool spot was in a house basement with the fans going.

The first curb service for Lawrence was probably started at Wiedemann's also. Wooden ladder-like frames, made especially for this, were placed across the back of the front seat of a car, and each end rested on the open window of the back doors. Orders were brought out on a tray which was placed on the rack. Curb service on Massachusetts street, yet!

Then came World War II. Wiedemann's again changed hands. Mr. John Parker became the next owner and shortly he went off to war. Sunflower Ordnance Works came—and help was attracted to the plant for higher wages than could be met in Lawrence. Supplies became increasingly hard to get. About 1943, Wiedemann's was sold at auction—truly a casualty of the war. And another mode of Lawrence living, died.

Printed in Journal-World Sept. 13, 1968

'Long Hairs' Not New
on Lawrence Horizon

WITH SO MUCH TALK THESE DAYS about long hair and beards, some of the older generation in Lawrence recall three outstanding examples that graced the streets of Lawrence during the early part of this century.

Of course, if one views the pictures of the early settlers in Lawrence, back in the 1860's, hair, beards, and clothes on the men resemble those to today in some circles. But that style changed for the majority, until the early 1900's when it cropped up in three men who were "different" from the establishment.

Naturally, they stood out and attracted lots of attention. The three were: Hugh H. Cameron, the Kansas Hermit; Harry Hibbard Kemp, the Tramp Poet; and Kirby McRill, who was called by some, the Sandwich Man.

Hugh Cameron came to Lawrence in July, 1854, but lived to age 81 and so came into the generation that had dropped the style of 1854. He was a free-state man and decided to come to Kansas where the action was. He is listed as a farmer in Andreas History of Kansas, 1883. His place was three miles north and west of Lawrence, on the south side of the Kansas River, and was designated as "Cameron Bluff."

He was born in New York state. Some dropouts might be interested to learn he did not go to school. He was self-educated. He did a good enough job of it, too, became a professor of mathematics at the Rittenhouse Academy in Washington, D. C. He didn't get to stay there too long as he was fired because he was linked with a close friend who was a radical. Later he "canvassed" for Harper's Magazine.

From there he came to Kansas. When the Civil War broke out, he enlisted and served two years in the 2nd Kansas Cavalry and came out a captain. He then served four years in the 2nd Arkansas Cavalry and came out a Lt. Colonel. In later years he was brevetted Brig. General of Volunteers for Meritorious services. He was called by many, "General Cameron."

The Hermit was a walker. All through the years, he walked to Washington to attend every inaugural ceremony. He had important friends in Washington. Webster and Clay were intimate friends. Politically, he was usually on the side of the minority. He printed a journal called "The Useful Worker" which was devoted to sobriety, equality and equity. As a writer, his style was bold and aggressive, and according to his contemporaries, these traits characterized his career in life. The journal did not last long. He also was a strong Prohibitionist.

People remember Cameron by his snow white flowing hair and long white bushy beard. Usually, he was dressed in a blue military coat with brass buttons, and in cold weather he wore an army blanket draped over his shoulders. Whenever a circus came to town, he would join the parade riding on a mule "with the Stars and Stripes draped gracefully around him."

There were two places where he lived. At the north end of Louisiana Street in the 500 block was a ravine. There he had built an open shack. It looked as though he had used the stone foundation and walls of a house that had been destroyed earlier. Perhaps burned in Quantrill's Raid? Leaning against a tall tree growing beside the shack was a long ladder reaching to a tree house.

An early picture postcard showing this scene is captioned Cameron's Bluff. But that is not correct. His abode at Cameron's Bluff was an old wooden piano box and on the outside of it was an iron boiler which he used as a cook stove.

The story goes, General Cameron did not like University students. That probably stemmed from the fact many students (boys and girls), would either walk up the Santa Fe tracks, or go by canoe or row boat, up the Kaw River, or walk the dusty, dirt road from Lawrence to the Bluff. This was a Saturday or Sunday pasttime and lark. The bold boys would approach Cameron and bother him and he would chase them off his property.

We were always a bit in awe of the Hermit and didn't venture to either of his homes. But some of the younger high school-age young people who lived nearby ventured to his shack on Louisiana Street. In fact, they worried that he might not be getting enough to eat and they would take him food. They always left right away, whether he was there or not. One time he wrote a poem to one of his benefactors and left it in the mail box at her home. It was entitled "The Angel." That's how her mother found out where the missing food from the ice box was going. Someone else remembered a poem he wrote that went like this:

"Jesus was in the wilderness 40 days, you know,
"And Foster fasted 40 days to make a splendid show;
"But I lay prostrate 7 weeks here — helpless and alone
"No wine to drink, no bread to eat — there was no telephone;
"Telephatic temple built of wood over a running stream —with
    no metal;
"Not even nails — put together with wooden pegs, so as not to
    deflect messages from the 'Prophet' in the Temple."

What changed Cameron into a hermit, no one seems to know. We used to speculate on why he became a recluse, such as perhaps an unrequited love affair. Now, to our astonishment, in reading about Mr. Cameron's death in 1907, we learned that a packet of love letters was found by some curious, young boys, who explored his shack on Louisiana Street, and found it hidden in the stone wall inside the shack. The packet contained letters addressed to a young woman by the name of Mary Phelps, sister of John E. Phelps who later became governor of Missouri. Miss Phelps had apparently returned them to Cameron.

The Hermit had two sisters who were living in Lawrence at the time of his death, but apparently he chose to live alone.

Harry Hibbard Kemp, the Tramp Poet, showed up in Lawrence in 1905. Although his hair was not extremely long, he still went bareheaded. The fact that he never wore a hat or cap, seemed to shake up both students and the town people. Besides that, he wore no socks. In the eyes of the community, his going around bareheaded caused more of a stir than his being a poet. His fellow students thought he thrived on being "different." In those days, that mode of dress was extremely unconventional. He is believed to have been the first student in Lawrence to go hatless.

He had the reputation among his fellow students of being a "free loader." He was likely to turn up at mealtime at any fraternity house or boarding house as a guest of a fellow student.

He came to Kansas from Ohio when he was three years old. The family came out to a farm near Hutchinson, where the grandfather lived, for Kemp's mother's health. In those early days, one reads often of people coming to Kansas to try to regain their health from tuberculosis. After the mother's death, the boy and his father returned to Ohio. In 1905, at age 22, he started out for Chicago to attend the University, when he got to thinking of his early life in Kansas. He also recalled a text book written by Wm. H. Carruth used in his German course at Mount Hermon, a boys school (where he had been expelled twice).

So, he hopped a freight train and arrived in Lawrence, broke. He looked up Prof. Carruth who befriended him and got him a job milking cows, (after Carruth's tutelage, and from which he was fired almost immediately).

As a KU student, Kemp spent many hours in Central Park writing poetry. On their way home from school, young grade school students would stop and talk to him. He was always friendly. Willard Wattles (a Kansas poet), was a student at KU then and he and Kemp were friends. Joe Murray, who later became managing editor of the Journal-World, was also a friend.

At that time, Mr. Murray was rooming at Prof. Sterling's. Where Kemp roomed is not certain. The Lawrence Directory of 1907 listed no residence address but gave his boarding address at 911 Mass. In 1911, he lived at the YMCA (the old Wren Building across the street from the present Standard Mutual Life building). This is a parking lot now.

.While at KU, Kemp wrote the following poem:

A Kansan's Choice

"Give me the land where miles of wheat
"Ripple beneath the wind's light feet.
"Where the green armies of the corn
"Sway in the first sweet breath of morn;
"Give me the large and liberal land
"Of the open heart and the generous hand;
"Under the wide-spread Kansas sky
"Let me live and let me die."

This poem was printed on a postcard with a sketch of a farm house and barn and fields surrounding. It seemed to have touched the hearts of many Kansans, as many have shown up in postcard albums.

After Kemp left Lawrence, he covered quite a bit of territory. Once he stowed away on a British liner to go to England, was caught and imprisoned. He adopted socialism and joined Upton Sinclair. But those ties were severed when he ran off with Sinclair's wife.

He joined Elbert Hubbard's colony but left because he said Hubbard had used one of his poems without giving Kemp's name. His correspondence shows letters from H. L. Menchen; Brock Pemberton; Walter Winchell; Fiorello LaGuardia; and Mrs. Eleanor Roosevelt's secretary. Some of these were letters acknowledging letters from him.

Kemp was a prolific writer. His works were published in text books, periodicals and newspapers; the New York Times being one of them. Some of the titles of his writings reflect his life: Tramping On Life (his autobiography); Poets Pilgrimage; House in the Sand; The Cape Enders, a novel;; and Songs from the Hill. He spent his last years in Provincetown, Mass., where he lived in a beach house on the dunes. There he was called the "Poet of the Dunes." He died at Provincetown in 1960.

Kirby McRill of Reno, Kan., was another "walker." He was described by many as the "Sandwich Man," as he was most often remembered wearing sandwich boards advertising some cafe in Kansas City. He always walked from his farm about three miles west of Reno, to Lawrence, Tonganoxie, Leavenworth or even Kansas City. He was a bachelor and a farmer, but he did not like to farm, so he ran a threshing machine outfit.

He wore heavy shoes which he claimed were given to him by the manufacturer, Endicott-Johnson. He wore a cowboy-type hat, crushed, long wool stockings and baseball-type pants, more generally known as knickerbockers. He was of sandy complexion and wore a handelbar mustache. When it was time to pay his taxes, he would walk to Leavenworth to pay them, a distance from his farm of about 20 miles.

One day, the story goes, someone stopped and offered to give him a lift. "No thanks," he said, "I'm in a hurry."

In those days, motorists often experienced flat tires and it took time to mend them on the road. Often when he walked to Tonganoxie and would arrive at noontime, he would stop in the bakery and buy a loaf of bread and a quart of ice cream and sit outside and eat it for his lunch. McRill spent his later years in Kansas City. He was described then as "Kirby, the Unkissed." At that time he had a red-dyed, heavy beard. And often could be seen tramping the streets of downtown Kansas City.

After these three men left Lawrence, there was a long, dry spell before long hair and beards showed up again — this time in considerably more volume.

War Nerves Blight German Role

ON THE CORNER OF NINTH AND RHODE ISLAND streets stands a massive stone building that belies its age. It is over 100 years old. A marker set near the top reads:

Lawrence
Turnhalle
1869

For 50 years this building and its Turnverein members, were in their prime, serving the German-American families in the community. Then 1917 and World War I changed everything. Today, after another 50 years, the sturdy, old building is again useful and appreciated. But in another way.

The Verein in Lawrence was organized in 1857. Their first hall was a large wooden structure at the corner of 10th and New York. The organization was patterened after the Vereins in Germany in some respects. In the old country, they were a political body and the members used physical fitness as a cover-up. Their primary interest was talking politics. In Lawrence, they were organized for physical fitness and sociability. As far as politics was concerned all shades of political opinions seemed to have been represented. Some were Republicans, some Democrats, but no one could recall that there were any Prohibitionists.

One of the requirements for membership in the Lawrence Verein was that the applicant must have taken out his first papers for citizenship in the United States. From 1857 to 1862, the membership flourished. Then, 1862 found the men enlisting in the Union Army. In fact, all but four members of the original group had enlisted. So the organization was forced to dissolve. In 1866, the society was reorganized and a charter was obtained from the State of Kansas, Jan. 7, 1869.

The charter showed the signatures of 25 men, among them were S. Steinbring; J. Oesch; P. Preisach; C. J. Walruff, who had a brewery and beer garden near the site of the Lawrence Memorial Hospital; William Zimmerman; F. J. Ecke, who was one of the organizers of the first group in 1857; and J. Planz.

During the summer of 1869, the present Turner Hall was built at a cost of $5,000, by members of the Turnverein Society. The hall became the social center for the many German families who had migrated to Lawrence. It also served as an employment center. Every Saturday, one would find many newcomers from the Fatherland on the steps of the Hall waiting for people to come and offer them jobs. The men were hired for their craftsmanship and the women were placed in homes as maids or housekeepers. They became substantial citizens of the community.

The interior of the stone structure was well planned. On the first floor was a fully equipped gymnasium. Attendance at gym practice was obligatory for all members between the ages of 18 and 30. One of the early "turning masters" was M. Heimann. Otto Rost was turning master around 1907 and on. There was keen rivalry between the gym teams and when competition matches were held, the spectators watched from a balcony at the west end of the building. That balcony is still standing and the sturdy railing looks like it could withstand many more spectators leaning on it.

There is a stage at the east end of the gymnasium where dramatic productions in German were presented. Adam Rohe, sign painter and artist, painted all of the scenery.

The basement was the daily social center. A long bar extending on the north wall dispensed beer on tap for adults and soda pop for children. You could also buy sandwiches. No hard liquor was served. Walnut card tables had slots under the tops for beer steins, while you sat in captains chairs and played pinochle or skat or other card games. Two bowling alleys were in use most of the time and children were allowed to use them too. The children set up their own pins.

A door near the east end of the bar led out to the beer garden in back. In warm weather this was a popular spot. It was lighted at night and there was a fence that enclosed it from the public. Sometimes a group of youngsters would go to the "Nickel" picture show in the 700 block of Massachusetts and after the show would walk down to the Hall to join their parents. They would come through the gate of the beer garden and knock on the window for the bartender to let them in . . .

Turner Hall had something to offer all ages. It was a family pleasure center. It was something the children shared with their parents. There were dances and masquerade parties and gymnaisum exhibitions and plays. Buch's Orchestra played in the early years for the dances and later, at the demands of the younger generation, Francis Saunders brought his orchestra down on the Santa Fe from Topeka to play the new dance music for the "Bunny Hug" and such "new" dances.

Elaborate costumes for the masquerades kept the dressmakers busy. Years later, on many rainy days, those costumes were dug out of camel-back trunks in the attic, for play. Wedding anniversaries were celebrated at the hall, and if it was a 25th, the Society presented the couple with a silver service. The dances always started with a Grand March and all its intricate patterns of marching were performed. Regardless of age, the children were encouraged to participate and dance. They were treated as adults by their elders and the men would bow and ask for a dance.

The smaller tots were put to bed in a room off the gymnasium where a "baby sitter" (an unheard of title then) watched over them. Some slept on gym pads spread out in back of the stage, while others slept on two chairs shoved together. On many of the nights of the family parties, William Reinisch (later our fire chief) would lead the singing by lifting his stein and the children would join in singing the old German drinking songs. At Christmas time, "Tannenbaum" was the favorite.

The annual Christmas tree party stands out. Tickets were sold for 25 cents for a drawing present from the tree. The gifts were donated by the merchants. Your ticket bore a number to be matched with one on the tree. A tree reaching to near the top of the ceiling was on the floor close to the stage. While "Tannenbaum" was being sung, Santa would appear in an opening in the ceiling above the stage and come down hand over hand on a rope to dispense more gifts from the tree.

It was no chore for Santa to come down in that fashion. All the men were experienced gymnasts.

In the heydey of the Turnverein, names of the members were: Adam Rohe, Kasold, Zimmerman, Gerhardt, Marks, Berger, Achning, Ernst, Barteldes, Graeber, Ketels, Urlaub, Fischer, Wilhelmi, Lahrman, Gnefkow, Thudium, Schleifer, Steinbring, Poehler, Smithmeyer, Jaedicke, Broemelsick, Willman, Wiedeman, Niemeyer, Hartig, Bell, Buch, Hetzel, Buermann, Reinisch, Lucken, Broeker and many more. As you read those names, you recall the many merchants whose names can still be seen on buildings on Massachusetts. They contributed to and stabilized the major part of the economy in Lawrence in those early years.

One day, word reached Lawrence, that Carry Nation was due to make a visit. Great preparations were made at Turner Hall for her reception should she invade their privacy with her hatchet to destroy their beer bar. A garden hose was attached near the bar. It was planned when she approached the bar, the bartender would turn on the hose full force and drench her. Fortunately for all concerned, when she arrived in Lawrence, Turner Hall was not on her itinerary.

World War I changed things drastically for the Verein. There was so much anti-feeling against the German-American in Lawrence, the organization felt forced to disband and close the building. This more or less came to a head by the death of William Wiedemann, the owner of the popular Wiedemann's candy and ice cream store.

After the war, things started up again, but the hall never regained its popularity. In 1938 the building was sold to Philip Ernst. The society retained a small lodge room, but Ernst leased the rest of the building to the Rumsey Vehicle Company where toys were manufactured for a short time. The national Guard then used it until their Armory was built. Next, the Salvation Army maintained an outlet store for several years.

Finally, the building was "discovered" by Ed Down, who saw its possibilities for his line of audio business.

Since 1965, Down has been renovating the interior. The walls and ceiling have been covered with plastic to keep out all dust. Not only is something of Old Lawrence being preserved, but bits of old KU as well. When you enter the building on East Ninth, which is now the "front door," you walk through a four-foot doorway. The wooden steps to the basement are flanked by a low stone wall made from stone taken from old Frazer Hall. At the foot of the stairs on each side is a bronze newel light lined in colored glass.

These lights came out of Blake Hall. On this floor, which is considered the first floor, is all of the studio equipment for cutting records. On the second floor, which was the gym floor, with its 18-foot ceiling, is used as an echo chamber.

Young people are once more enjoying it. A basketball net has been installed at the west end below the balcony. This makes a good practice court for the 6th grader in the family, and his friends. Some of the other Down youths hold dances there and the stage holds the band.

So, once again Turner Hall is being used for youth, music and exercise and from all visible appearances, is good for at least another 100 years.

Printed in Journal-World April 28, 1971

Christmas Vacation Times

ARE STUDENTS TODAY AS frivolous and carefree and gay as they were 50 years ago? Every year when the holiday season is at hand and Christmas vacation starts at Kansas University, one is reminded of those past times. When the last class was dismissed, all thoughts of school were put aside for two weeks. No one planned to catch up with reading at the library or sought to complete lab work. There were too many more "important" things going on. No trips to Mexico, or to Colorado for skiing, were in the picture. No one wanted to leave town for the holidays because you had too much fun in Lawrence. Besides, holiday diversions were unheard of then.

Two weeks before vacation time, fraternities and sororities set the pace for things to come. Dances, either at the house or in Ecke's or Fraternal Aid Union Hall, were held. The Betas had their "German", the Phi Gams their "Pig Dinner", and the Phi Psis their Christmas party. Formal, engraved invitations were sent out. Elaborate five and six course dinners were served. Menus were printed, as were the dance programs. At one such party, a song was sung between each course and the song to be sung had the words printed on the menu.

The menu: Oyster cocktail — song — Cream Tomato Soup — Celery, olives, cheese straws — song — Roast Turkey, oyster dressing, June peas, Mashed potatoes, cranberry sauce, Sandwiches (?) — song — Waldorf salad — song — Cafe Parfait, Cake, Candies — song — coffee — song. At that time, the Phi Kappa Psi fraternity had 18 actives and 8 pledges and the party was at the Fraternal Aid Union Hall. A good many of the fraternities gave favors at these parties. What they were was always kept a secret until the big night. It might be a lavaliere of the fraternity crest, or a silver mesh purse.

Christmas tree parties the Sunday before vacation recess were held at the houses, too. At the Sigma Chi house an informal supper preceded the gift distribution. Mrs. Petty was the housemother. The gifts were always jokes on the receivers, with a poem that had to be read aloud to the group. After that, the evening was spent sitting on the floor around the tree and singing Christmas songs.

After the out-of-town students had left Lawrence, it was time for the Lawrence young people to get together.

During school time, you were busy with your own particular groups, but vacation time brought everybody together again, regardless of club affiliations. Dancing, skating, and coasting were the main activities. There were "tea" dances or "matinee" dances in Ecke's Hall, (above where Duckwall's downtown store is now). That dance floor had two springs under it so that when you danced, or even walked across it, it would "give" in rhythm. Fraternal Aid Union Hall had three springs under their floor. These matinee dances were subscription affairs, as were the "varsity" dances in the evenings. The boys usually paid 50 cents a couple. If the group was to be small, sometimes the dance would be held in IOOF Hall (upstairs and across the street from the Fire Department on 8th and Vermont). Sometimes the boys engaged Eagles Hall on East Warren.

The music for the dances in the halls, was always "live" and consisted usually of a piano and banjo. One popular pair to play was "Swede and Eric", (Swede Wilson and Eric Owens). Swede played the banjo and Eric the piano. They were paid around $5 for the evening. If the dancers wanted to dance after midnight, the boys would chip in and collect a dollar or two more, for an extra hour's music. The players always seemed to enjoy their work as much as the dancers enjoyed it. And if you asked them to play a special favorite number, they always obliged willingly. Sometimes the orchestra was increased to three by adding Swede's brother, Al Wilson, who also played the banjo. Then there was "Shanty" Newhouse and his orchestra. He always had at least three in his group, and one would be a violinist.

At smaller functions and at fraternity houses, Baldwin Mitchell, (the late A. B. Mitchell), former attorney general of Kansas, and father of Dr. Alex Mitchell) was a popular piano player. He would get $3 a night and sometimes only $2. "Honey" Warfield, a happy-go-lucky Lawrence Negro, was also a popular piano player.

If you were at a dance downtown, at intermission you usually walked to Chris Epley's on the east side of Massachusetts Street in the 700 block, for oyster stew for which you could have a small bowl for 15 cents, or a large one for a quarter. Or you would go to Wiedemann's (about where the Jay Shoppe is now), and eat chili for 10 cents or drink hot chocolate with a marshmallow on top, for 5 cents, or an ice cream soda for 10 cents. The rich ice cream, of course, was made by Wiedemanns.

Sometimes parents would give formal dances for a son or daughter, and these would be held in Ecke's Hall. You walked to these functions, your date carrying your dancing slippers in your velvet slipper bag, or one that matched your party coat. Very rarely did you take a hack (horse drawn) for 25 cents. There were several livery stables to choose from; Donnelly's at the corner of Seventh and New Hampshire; Moak's, back of the Eldridge Hotel; Francisco's, about the middle of the 800 block on Vermont Street on the east side; and Chris Hunsinger's place of business at 922 Massachusetts, where it was established in 1901.

When you arrived at a formal party, there was always a receiving line. The Grand March started at 9:30 and there was a five-piece orchestra. At 11 o'clock, a light lunch was served.

The big event of the holiday season, was the annual "bunch" dance held in Ecke's Hall on New Year's Eve. We believe it was originally started by a group of high school boys belonging to a high school fraternity called the "Delts", (Delta Omicron Omicron). Each year the same boys promoted it. It was a money making deal for them, but you had to be asked to come, even if you had to pay your dollar to get in. It later became so popular, it finally was held in Fraternal Aid Union Hall. This was the largest hall in Lawrence. It was where the present Standard Life building now stands. With three springs in those floors, we wonder what the twist and some of the newer dances would have done to the resilient wood surface. Someone recalled that one night they were dancing the barn dance and the floor was swinging. The janitor came in and asked what was going on and they told him they were dancing the Barn dance. He expostulated—"Hell, this ain't no barn".

Most of the dance programs listed the names of the dances that were to be played, such as: "1-Waltz—For You Dear Heart"; "2-Two Step—Mr. Moon Turn Off Your Lights". The last number (there would be 18 or 20 listed, and sometimes a place for "extras"), was always "Aloha" or "Good Night Ladies".

Waltzes seemed to be the most popular. One program shows 12 waltzes and 6 two-steps. On a 1915 dance program, the new steps were coming in and were reflected on the programs; such as: One Step; Canter; Fox Trot; The Boston; Castle Walk; Fish Walk; Hesitation Waltz. And you danced only the type dance designated for that particular number.

The "Phi Gam Corner" was a popular variation, originating at the local Phi Gam frat house. P. J. Cubbison was one of the best dancers for that improvised step. You could dance it either with a waltz or two-step. All you did was when you came to a corner, the boy backed the girl in and hesitated a beat or two, then she came forward and the boy backed out.

In the daytime, you went skating on the river, or maybe there was a tea dance or matinee. Interspersed with all this, would be coasting parties and Victrola parties at two of the most frequently used and open fraternity houses; the Phi Psi house, then at 1140 Louisiana and the Alpha Tau Omega House at 1633 Vermont. Everybody went, regardless of their affiliations. You always had to make sure there were to be chaperones before you were allowed to go. No food was served. You always walked to town for that.

The Betas and the Phi Psis had the two biggest bob-sleds for coasting. They would hold from 16 to 18 people. There was always a big husky boy to guide, usually "Lefty" Sproull, or Ray Folks, or "Stuffy" Dunmire, on the Phi Psi sled. One boy always sat on the end in case of a spill. Indiana Street was the most popular hill for the Phi Psis and the Betas used 14th Street, then called Adams. You yelled all the way down to warn sleighs and hacks to clear the intersections. After several serious spills with resulting broken bones, skull fractures, and a fatality, and before the City passed an ordinance prohibiting coasting down the hill, one boy was posted at the intersection of 9th and Indiana to stop traffic until you coasted by. By the time you reached 8th and Indiana, you had gained tremendous speed and could make it, with a full load on the sled, to the Water-Works at the foot of Indiana. The boys clocked it once and the sled gained a speed of 60 miles an hour. If you coasted down 14th Street, you ended up at the cemetery—alive. A boy was posted at the intersection of 14th and Tennessee, as this was the most dangerous intersection.

You didn't mind the long, cold, slippery walk back up the hill, because it was so exciting. You were warmly dressed in several sweaters, long stockings, skirt (no slacks in those days), a stocking cap down over your ears, long winter "undies", a long warm coat, high leather boots that had been vulcanized, or galoshes over high-top shoes, and of course, warm mittens, and sometimes two pairs of those. However, after two or three trips down, you were ready to walk over to the Phi Psi house to get warmed up, and to dance to Victrola records. If not enough couples showed up to fill the bobsled, you walked to town to the "Nickel" or Patee's movie theatre (about where the J. C. Penney store is now) and paid a nickel admittance.

When you went skating on the river, you wore about the same type and amount of clothes you did for coasting. The snow was swept off the ice and a rink formed, usually near the foot of Ohio Street. Our skates were the clamp-on kind. "Shoe" skates were unheard of then. Sometimes the channel of the river was next to the shore and the water would be running swiftly. Then a narrow plank would be bridged across to reach the ice rink. One memorable Sunday afternoon, one of the girls lost her balance and toppled over into the icy water. The boy next to her, grabbed her by the hair and held her up until she could be lifted out by the others. It didn't mar the afternoon's sport, however. She ran on home a couple of blocks away, changed, and was ready to greet us when we stopped in for tea and Christmas cookies on our way home.

Printed in Journal-World Dec. 19, 1964

Lawrence the Beautiful

LAWRENCE THE BEAUTIFUL! It is generally conceded that Lawrence is truly a beautiful city. Compare her to the atributes of a beautiful woman. She has culture, is religious, has a good appearance and is well liked and admired by many.

But Lawrence was not always like she is today. And it is well to recall the past to appreciate the present. She was born in 1854 (116 years ago), came of good stock and background. Members of the New England Emigrant Aid Society came to Kansas to encourage persons with anti-slavery convictions to settle here in an effort to assure the admittance of Kansas to the Union as a free state. Many of her other relatives were from Germany and they contributed stability to the economy of the town.

When Lawrence was first settled, there were few trees—and these probably were the red bud, wild cherry, paw paw, persimmon, black walnut and perhaps native pine. The homes were ugly tents and rough structures, but to offset this, there were beautiful wild flowers, wild birds and animals and a beautiful Kaw River. Some of the wild flowers were the sunflower, Kansas gay feather, wild verbena, wild larkspur, johnny-jump-ups, dog tooth violet, wild pansy and many more.

From Mount Oread there was and still is one of the most beautiful sights to see anywhere. On the south, the Wakarusa River and then the hills of Pleasant Grove. And now at night, the many thousands of lights, all colors, of the thousands of homes.

To the north of Mount Oread are the Kaw River and then the hills. Dr. Edward Baumgardner wrote an article on trees for the Journal-World some years ago and in it he said, "When the settlers first came, there were some large trees on the north side of the river. There was a large cottonwood at the north end of New Hampshire near the Paper Mill where the Sand Bank Convention was held—July 17, 1855. Strips of timber extended up all the ravines some distance from the river. There was a spreading oak south of the First Baptist Church, and a shellbark hickory on the northeast corner of Ohio and 8th".

Dr. Baumgardner said tree planting started in the late 1860's and he mentioned hackberry—3 trees planted a block south of the new Woodlawn School (North Lawrence) and Elm trees in Bismarck Grove—burr oak, red oak and chestnut oak. A soft maple was planted on the Robinson farm in 1863. The trees in the 1100 block of Tennessee were planted the day of Lincoln's assassination.

My grandparents planted the elm trees at 743 Indiana sometime in the 1879 or 80's and last summer the last one was cut down, a victim of elm disease. Its base measured over three feet across.

Dr. Baumgardner also wrote that a "dense forest covered the site of North Lawrence". From my reading I would question the "dense". I well remember the walnut groves near where the highway intersection parts at the Tee Pee. We used to gather walnuts there and many other spots in North Lawrence. Speaking of walnut groves, I recently ran across an invitation to the opening of a new hospital "Walnut Park", North Lawrence, September 17, 1892.

But let us go back again to those earliest times in Lawrence. The people endured many hardships to make Lawrence what it is today. They suffered being burned out by raiders—the pro-slavery men—and then Quantrill's Raid. They survived the grasshopper scourge—the flood of 1903—and the tornado in 1911—then another devastating flood in 1951. But each time they made it back by determined effort and working together for a common cause. These early settlers had faith in themselves and in the future, and divine faith to start all over again.

Perhaps this is more or less the history of all early Kansas towns. In those days, the threats to Lawrence seemed to be mostly physical—today, are we being threatened again? And are we being undermined spiritually?

Typical of the character of these early settlers, the men constructed a church before they began to build their own homes.

Plymouth Congregational Church was the first. The first sermon was preached by Rev. Lum in 1854. This was seven years before Kansas became a state. All through the years, Plymouth has been a strong influence in Lawrence, not only spiritually, but culturally and civically.

Lawrence didn't jump right from tents and crude structures to beautiful homes. Downtown, we have gone through the stage of a motley array of feed stores, blacksmith shops, grocery stores and meat markets, livery stables, candy kitchens, saloons and a brewery. We had board walks, then brick walks, mud streets, then brick paving before the blacktop and concrete. There was a sign that hung over the Kaw River Bridge that referred to an ordinance passed in 1902 that read: "5 dollars fine for riding or driving over this bridge faster than a walk". And on some of the brick sidewalks was embedded in each brick, "Don't spit on the sidewalk". Bricks that now sell in antique shops for $8-$9 each.

A good many of us know about Lawrence and its past, but how many of us know about Lawrence as it is today? Lawrence now has 50 Protestant churches, 1 Catholic, 1 Jewish, 18 grade schools, 3 junior highs, 1 senior high and 1 parochial school. It has the University of Kansas with 18,000 students, and Haskell Institute which was founded in 1884. Haskell was designated a National Historic Landmark by the U. S. National Park Service in 1962. It now provides vocational and academic opportunities for representatives of 126 tribes from 36 states. It has facilities